Estate Inventories

How To Use Them

By Kenneth L. Smith

ESTATE INVENTORIES
HOW TO USE THEM

Library of Congress Number: 00-131603
International Standard Book Number: 1-930353-10-3

Printed 2000 by
Masthof Press
220 Mill Road
Morgantown, PA 19543-9701

CONTENTS

TABLES

PREFACE

As was the case with my previous book on dating systems, this book has arisen from difficulties I have encountered in my own research, for which I was unable to find any published materials that could be of help. The materials that were available were scattered throughout hundreds of different books, many of which were available only in large reference libraries. Needless to say, I did a great deal of traveling. It is hoped that this book will fill that void.

Out of necessity, the scope of this work is somewhat limited. It will deal only with inventories in the English language. The material is intended to apply primarily to the United States and Colonial America, but it often applies equally well to inventories from any English-speaking country. Although no conscious effort was made to restrict the material temporally, the bulk of the documents used in its preparation dated no earlier than 1600 and very few postdated 1900. It was felt that few people are likely to have to deal with inventories from before the seventeenth century and that materials from after 1900 are usually understood without too much trouble.

While an attempt was made to study documents from various geographical regions of the United States, it must be admitted that the author's personal experience has centered primarily on Ohio, Pennsylvania, and Virginia.

Kenneth L. Smith
4936 Whisper Cove Ct.
Columbus, OH 43230

INTRODUCTION

It is amazing how many genealogical researchers completely ignore estate inventories. These same people would not dream of not checking for a will or for records of the settlement or partition of an estate, but inventories? Who cares? Sure, it's nice to know how many hogs Great-grandpa owned, but this is hardly indispensable information. While it is true that inventories are not as likely to give information on family relationships (although they sometimes do), they can often give something that is, to some people, even more valuable.

For those interested strictly in establishing as many family lines as possible and in extending those lines as far back as possible, inventories are not particularly fertile fields to plow. But for those who, like most of us, are as much interested in family history as in genealogy, they yield glimpses into the personal lives of our ancestors. Diaries and personal correspondence can certainly provide better views into day-to-day lives, but such documents rarely survive, if indeed they ever existed at all. Estate inventories, on the other hand, are very often extant and, when viewed through astute eyes, they can offer much information of the same genre.

In the opening chapter to one of his books, Ivor Noël Hume, the noted Williamsburg, Virginia, archaeologist, mentions that one of his "more curious friends" (I'm still not sure whether "curious" means "having curiosity" or "strange. "), when visiting a strange house, always makes it a point to look into the bathroom closet, claiming that it gives him great insight into the everyday nature of the household.[1] Estate inventories allow the researcher a furtive peek into closets that have remained closed for many years. Consider your own situation: how much could someone infer about your personal interests, likes, and dislikes by studying a listing of the items in the room in which you spend the bulk of your time at home?

It is the purpose of this book to help you get as much as possible out of the studying of the inventories of the personal possessions of your forebears. The more obvious matters, such as simply figuring out what they say, will, of course, be covered. But we will not restrict ourselves to the mundane. Other parts of the book will put forth ideas on how inferences can be drawn from what is presented in the listing, so that you can get a more enlightening peek into the bathroom closet.

---

[1] Ivor Noël Hume, *A Guide to Artifacts of Colonial America*, (N.Y.: Alfred A. Knopf, Inc., 1969). p. 29.

CHAPTER 1

WHAT DOES IT SAY?

Before one can indulge in the esoteric, he must master the mundane. The first (and often the most difficult) task facing the researcher is that of figuring out what the inventory says. Since it has been stated that we are restricting ourselves to inventories written in the English language, this would at first consideration seem patently obvious, but after one has examined a few inventories, it no longer seems so simple. There are several reasons for the problem, not the least of which is that these documents are invariably handwritten, but the solution to all of them lies primarily in patience and perseverance.

Structure

The first thing to consider is that all inventories have some kind of structure. This is not to say that they all have the same structure, but most of them do have some aspects in common. They usually begin with a paragraph similar to this:

> *An Appraisment of the several goods and chattels of Michael Frase of Forks Township in the County of Northampton, Deceased—made this 19th Day of June in the year of our Lord 1828.*

Other examples might give more or less information, but in general the introductory statement will at least give the name of the deceased and usually the location and date. A similar statement generally appears at the end of the inventory. That corresponding to the example given above was:

> *Appraised By us—June the 19th, 1828. Sworn and Subscribed before me . . . Jacob Kämmer*
>
> *George Brinker*
> *Georg Lerch [German script]*

This concluding statement supplies in this example the other information that is inevitably included: the name(s) of the person/people who made the inventory and the name of the representative of the court who accepted it. There are some cases in which all the information is to be found as a single paragraph either at the beginning or at the end.

The genealogical information to be gleaned from this simple paragraph is not insignificant. One could conclude that the Michael Frase in the above example died before June 19, 1828, and probably not too long before that date—almost certainly in 1828. In the absence of death or burial records, this at least gives an approximate death date. One can also learn from this example that Michael Frase lived not only in Northampton County, but specifically in Forks Township. Some early census records do not break counties down into townships (or towns or parishes), especially in sparsely settled rural areas.

An additional hint toward location is given in the names of those who made the inventory. It was customary for a relative or a neighbor to be assigned this task. It is also worth noting that one of the inventoriers signed his name in German script (note also that the other inventorier has a German surname). Although this may or may not reveal anything of genealogical importance, it does give a clue that may help in deciphering unclear entries in the list: German phonetics may creep into the spellings used. This particular problem is covered in more detail later.

The internal structure of the inventories may vary more greatly; it seems to have depended on the length and complexity of the listings more than on anything else. Simple, short inventories may just have everything thrown together in an apparent hodgepodge. However, there is usually some rational order to the entries, if for no other reason than that the inventoriers usually went through the house room by room, listing items as they went.

This same method of organization is often formalized in longer inventories, with items being listed under actual headings, stating in which rooms they were found. In some other instances, the items are grouped according to how they were to be distributed among the heirs. This is a particularly nice situation when it occurs, since in the absence of a will one can assume that those named were the legal heirs of the deceased. On the other end of the spectrum are those inventories in which the entries are not even broken down into lines, but rather are presented as a solid block of data.

Since the inventory was taken to give the court settling the estate an idea of the financial worth of the deceased, other money-related items are frequently listed, even though they were not physical items. Most often these include notes (debts) owed to and by the deceased. These are generally found at the end or the beginning.

Similar to these are the so-called "book accounts" that one occasionally finds. They also refer to money loaned by the deceased, but there was no formal, written agreement signed by the parties involved, as would be the case with notes or bonds. A notation was simply made in the loaner's personal account book. One may assume the loaner expected no difficulty in recovering his money. For this reason, people listed in these book accounts were very often related to the loaner.

There are often listings of money that had been given to children during the lifetime of the deceased. These were not debts in the sense that they were to be repaid, but rather a portion of his inheritance-to-be given to the child when he was establishing a home of his own and had need of financial assistance. They are listed because they were considered a portion of the estate, as it would have been had they not been given earlier, and so that they could be deducted from that child's share of the final estate. Occasionally, one also finds listings of expenses to be met out of the estate, such as funeral costs, physicians' bills, court costs, etc. Again, these are usually grouped, but it seems to have been a matter of personal preference as to exactly where they appear.

The assigning of values to the individual items was done in two ways. More commonly, several items are grouped in one line (and the word "sundries" seems ubiquitous) with a net value assigned to the group. In other cases, each item within a group is assigned a value and the total appears at the end of the line. There are some inventories that combine both of these methods, grouping many items and assigning a net value while breaking down others, especially where crops were involved (they give a per bushel value as well as a net value). In some instances, two values are given for each entry: one is an appraised value and the other is what the items mentioned actually fetched at auction. It should be noted, however, the fact that an inventory of the estate was made does not necessarily imply that the items were to be auctioned. Frequently there is a summary of debits and credits at the end and a statement of the net appraised value of the estate. This is more commonly found in longer, more complex inventories, but it is not restricted to them any more than it is an integral part of them.

Writing

Simple legibility is often the single greatest problem in interpreting inventories. If one cannot make out the individual letters that go together to form the words, the words and hence the meanings cannot be ascertained, either. Problems of legibility emanate from three primary sources.

Anything written in haste is likely at least to border on illegibility. Despite common jokes to the contrary, medical students do not have to prove they have sloppy handwriting or be forced to take a course to develop it. Physicians have a great deal of writing to do, and they are usually rushed—your last prescription, which appeared to be written in Sanskrit, was the result. This problem seems to have been common among inventoriers as well, since some of the most horrible script is to be found in those inventories which survive as they were originally taken. Inventories found in book form are more likely to be readable, since they are usually transcriptions of the originals as made by court clerks. Unfortunately, even some of those in ledger books hardly qualify as the epitome of the calligrapher's art.

When one encounters a poorly written inventory, there is really only so much one can do. There are times when the final two-thirds of words simply degenerate into a wavy line, or the words appear as smudged globs. This latter instance frequently occurs in older inventories which were written with a quill that was not sharpened often enough.

Completely hopeless cases are not usual, but they do occur. More commonly encountered is the situation in which most of the material is legible, but occasional difficulties present themselves. Some of these will fall into the category mentioned above, and they may indeed be hopeless. Many times, however, these words are problems because of factors which can be overcome with a little effort. The more common reasons for a potentially readable word to appear unreadable are the use of now archaic forms of script, idiosyncrasies of a particular inventorier in forming some of his letters, and the use of terms that are now archaic, obsolete, or a part of the jargon of an occupation with which the reader is unfamiliar.

There are only a few different (although in common use at the time) conventions of script that one is likely to encounter in American inventories. The one with which most researchers are already familiar is the so-called long s. It is most commonly encountered as the first s in a double-s construction, but it is not necessarily restricted to this situation. The example on the next page contains two examples of the long s: "dresser" in line 3 and "glass" in line 4.

Another construction frequently seen is the reflexed d, in which the stem is brought back to the left instead of being made nearly vertical. It looks something like the symbol ∂. Depending on the writer, it may be found for all d's or only for final d. The stem may extend well back across the word, and it is important not to mistake it for the crossing of t's.

To point out how not recognizing this construction can lead to disaster, let me recount a problem I met in my own research. For

An example from an inventory from Pickaway County, Ohio, demonstrating some peculiarities of script. Long-s constructions are found in lines 3 and 4 and a reflexed d in line 2. Note similarity between S (line 6) and L (lines 1 and 4), and the similarities between double-s (3,4) and p (2,7).

years I looked without success for a family named Battott in Virginia; every reference I found gave the same spelling. When I finally realized that every material in which I had encountered the name could be traced back to a single source (a DAR application), I tried to track down the original material for this application. The reference was finally located in a family Bible, in which the name was found written:

If one recognizes the final letter as a reflexed *d*, the name easily resolves itself into Ballard. A somewhat poor example of this type of *d* is found in the previous example. In some earlier records one may encounter the use of the same letter for both *i* and *j*, as well as a single letter for both *u* and *v*. Unlike the previous two constructions, this one occurs in both upper and lower case forms. Finally, there are some letters and combinations of letters that often look alike in script. Some of the more common ones are given at the top of the next page.

Script Look-alikes

Since the problem of very different forms of script is relatively uncommon in American inventories after 1700, and since the matter of Middle English scripts is complex enough to merit a book on it alone, no detailed discussion is presented here. Those who encounter the problem are referred to either Val D. Greenwood, *The Researcher's Guide to American Genealogy* (Baltimore: Genealogical Publishing Company, 1978), Chapter 2; or E. Kay Kirkham, *The Handwriting of American Records for a Period of 300 Years* (Logan, Utah: Everton Publishing, 1973).

Individual peculiarities of script must be dealt with in situ. The matter is best resolved by looking elsewhere in the inventory for another word in which the same symbol appears and in which its meaning can be determined. Finding it in proper names can often give the greatest help, since it is usually obvious what the word is intended to be. For example, of the odd symbol is found as the fifth letter in the name Geor_e, it must represent lower case *g*. This conclusion should be cross-checked by looking in other words, enough of which are readable to determine that they must contain the letter in question.

In very difficult cases, it may be necessary to construct an entire alphabet of the inventorier's letters. An example of an oddly formed letter is the lower case *b* in the previous sample inventory (lines 1 and 7). It looks more like an upper case *C*, but the context makes it clear that it must be a *b*. It should also be noted that not everyone makes the same letter the same way each time he writes it. A difference is frequently seen between the way a letter is made within a word and the way it is made at the end of a word. Consider the *r*'s and *t*'s in the following words:

Spelling

Many of you probably find yourselves in the same situation as I when it comes to spelling—I can't, at least not with any consistency. I am equally certain that those of you who share this affliction were beset throughout your school years by teachers who had little sympathy for you. Well, the time for hair shirts is over. The spelling of English words has been standardized for a relatively short period of time. Prior to the advent of broad-scale public education, people were basically free to spell words as they saw fit; as long as the reader could decipher the word, the spelling was acceptable.

Although spelling words in variance to the currently accepted standards should not cast aspersions on the intelligence of the writer, it does cause problems for those of us who have been reared under the ideal of "one word, one spelling." We have been trained to recognize a word in only one form. There is, however, one saving principle underlying how words in inventories, however garbled they may seem, were constructed. They are invariably spelled phonetically. With this in mind, one would think it a relatively simple matter to figure them out. This would indeed be true if it were not for a few monkey wrenches in the linguistic works.

The first of these problems is that not all people pronounce the same word the same way. This fact is usually attributable to dialectic and accent variations, or to simple sloppiness on the part of the speaker. The other two factors are somewhat intertwined, albeit remotely: they both deal with the influence of non-English languages.

Most native speakers of a language can recognize when someone else speaks with an accent, even if they cannot necessarily localize its origin. When accents become too different from the parent pronunciation, one is beginning to deal with dialectic variation.[2] To someone spelling phonetically, accent or dialectic variation in pronunciation invariably leads to differences in spelling. As pointed out earlier, this same phenomenon can also result from simple sloppiness in pronunciation. To illustrate

---

[2] In general, it has been taken axiomatically here that accent variation consists of such things as modification of vowel sounds (rounding, flattening, etc.) and certain other minor modifications in pronunciation (e.g. the tendency of Bostonians to pronounce a final *a* as an *er*). When heavier modifications in consonant structure, actual substitution of vowels, and the addition of new words (or the changing of the meanings and/or connotations of existing words) begin, the forms of the language have become dialects.

[3] Although I realize many would disagree, I am considering British and American English to be dialects of the same language. While it is granted that they do not differ from each other to the extent that, for example, German dialects do, there is a greater difference between them than can be attributed to accent variation alone. The distinction between accents and dialects is a subjective one, and I have no desire to become bogged down in the debate, since it digresses from the real matter at hand.

these problems, the following examples, taken from various inventories, are provided:

1 plough
1 gal. Ertenware wit Sundries
4 Kitching chaires

In the first example, the standard British spelling for the American "plow" has been used. Both spellings are correct. They merely demonstrate that British and American English do not spell all words common to both dialects[3] the same way. This is discussed in more detail below. The second example reflects accent variation: use of *t* instead of *th* in "earthenware" and "with." It is taken from an inventory made by a Pennsylvania German. German does not have a *th* sound that is distinguishable from a *t* sound.

The third example shows, in a somewhat reverse manner, sloppiness in pronunciation. Since the person apparently knew that words he commonly heard as ending in *-in* (such as "comin'" and "goin'") were actually spelled with *-ing*, he extrapolated that any word ending in an *-in* sound (as "kitchen") should also be spelled with *-ing*.

Although there is no question that written British and American English are each understandable to a reader of the other dialect, there are some differences as to how words common to both forms are spelled. There is, fortunately, some consistency as to how they differ. American words ending in *-or* are usually spelled *-our* in the British form, and American words ending in *-er* are sometimes rendered in British as *-re*. Examples of these would be *color/colour* and *center/centre*. British also sometimes uses *s* where American uses *z* in words like *civilization/civilisation*. As the previous example demonstrated, the British sometimes spell the sound *ow* (rhymes with "now") as *ough*.

There is one tendency in British English, however, that is not really paralleled in American: the shortening of words, especially proper names, in order to reduce the number of syllables to one or two. This is not particularly difficult to handle in those cases where the word has basically been truncated, but it is also accomplished through slurring of internal syllables. It should be noted, however, that the formal spelling often remains unchanged, despite the slurred pronunciation. This leads to problems when the words are phonetically spelled, since this spelling often bears little resemblance to the original. Two examples of this are *Leicester* and *Gloucester*, pronounced respectively as if spelled *Lester* and *Gloster*. But if this tendency is applied primarily to proper names, does it really matter that much to someone trying to decipher an inventory?

Place names are often used as adjectives to specify a certain type of a particular item or, if the place is sufficiently famous for a particular product, the place may stand for the item. The following examples are taken from the inventory of the estate of Lord Botetort (Governor of Virginia, 1768-1770):

> *4 Staffordsh^e coffee pots*
> *1 Sheffield ware tea Kitchen*
> *11 Chelsea china figures*

In this example, all the proper nouns are used as adjectives, but there are times when they stand alone. Place names not associated with Great Britain or America are also used in the same way, but in this case the garbling of the spelling is not due to dialectic variation, but rather to the fact that most inventoriers had no idea how these place names were actually spelled. The problem is compounded when the place name contains sounds not found in English; for example, Osnabrück (a type of coarse linen produced in the German town of that name; English corruption: Osnaburg) is often found as "Oznabrig."

English is a language basically of Germanic stock; indeed, it belongs linguistically to the Germanic branch of the Indo-European family of languages. It has, however, felt heavier foreign influences than many other languages. These have come primarily from French (brought by the Normans in 1066) and Latin (the international language from the Middle Ages until a few centuries ago).

The incorporation of many words of foreign origin into the language has resulted, at least indirectly, in the simultaneous incorporation of the phonetic systems of those languages. This has served to make the correct spelling of English words dependent on one's memorization abilities or a keen knowledge of the etymologies of the words. The ultimate result of this influence has been to provide English with a number of remarkably varied ways in which to spell the same sound. This does not mean that combinations of French origin, for example, are used only in words of French origin. For someone spelling phonetically, if a certain combination of letters is used for a certain sound in one word, it may be used for that same sound in any other word, regardless of whether or not the words derive from the same language. For example, such a person might spell the word *daytime* as *deztime,* since *dez* has the sound of d$\bar{a}$ in the word *rendezvous,* even though one word is of French origin and the other Germanic.

To put the specifics into a more practically useful format, the following points usually apply:

1) Variation in consonants is unusual, but does occur. There are simply not as many possibilities as with vowel sounds. There is one major exception to this, but it is a special case and is discussed later. Some consonants occur in pairs, one form being voiced and the other unvoiced. The difference is whether one makes a sound with the vocal cords or not when saying the sound; the position of the lips and tongue is the same. These consonants are:

Voiced		Unvoiced	
Letter	*Example*	*Letter*	*Example*
b	bay	p	pay
d	dent	t	tent
f	ferry	v	very
s	sap	z	zap

Such pairs are sometimes used interchangeably. Some consonant sounds can also be given by another consonant or groups of consonants.

Equivalent Sounds

Sound	*Example*	*Also Spelled*	*Example*
soft c	cite	s	site
hard c	metric	k, ck	make, tick
f	stuff	ph, gh	glyph, rough
soft g	gesture	j	jest
n	nice	kn, gn	knife, gnome
m	rum	mn	autumn
x	tax	ks, cs, cks	talks, tics, tacks
(t) z	blitz	ts	bits
ch	chef	sh	sherry

Note that the equivalencies given above could be applied in either direction; that is, *rum* could be spelled *rumn* or *autumn* as *autum*. Consonants are often indiscriminately doubled or left single.

2) Short vowels seem to be interchanged with total abandon and are sometimes replaced by diphthongs (loosely, a combination of vowels in a single syllable pronounced as one sound by slurring).

3) Long vowel sounds also appear in many different spellings, but there is generally a little more rationality evident in these spellings than in short vowel substitutions. The listing below gives some of the various ways each long vowel sound can be spelled. This list does not pretend to be

exhaustive, but should serve to apprise the reader of some of the more common possibilities.

Sound	Spellings	Example
long a	a	state
	ai	bait
	au	gauge
	ay	stay
	ea	great
	ei	feint
	ey	they
long e	e	meteor
	ea	flea
	ee	feet
	ei	receive
	i	curious
	i_e	carbine
	ie	thief
	(e) y	monkey, mighty
long i	i	kite
	aye	aye
	eye	eye
	(e) igh	neigh, sigh
	ie	pie
	uy	buy
	ye	bye
	y	my
long o	o	smote
	oe	hoe
	ough	furlough
	ow	arrow
long u	u	mute
	ew	flew
	eu	pneumonia
	oo	toot
	ou	route
	ui	fruit
	ue	glue
	uu	vacuum

diphthong

ou	ou	about
	ow	cow

diphthong

oi	oi	boil
	oy	boy

Mention was made earlier of a special case regarding the influence of non-English languages on spelling. In this instance, English words, regardless of their etymologies, are spelled according to a foreign phonetic system. It usually arises when the inventorier was not a native speaker of English and, more specifically, when he received his basic education in another language. When such a person learned to spell, he did so under the phonetic rules of the language he was using at the time. Consequently, when he later encountered English words, the spellings of which he was uncertain, he spelled them by sound. Unfortunately (for us), he used the letter combinations he had learned in school as representative of those sounds.

The same letter combinations do not denote the same sound in all languages, even those that use the same alphabet. In American records one encounters most often the phonetic systems of three non-English languages: German, French, and Spanish. In the material which follows, the spelling of the non-English language is given, followed by the English letter(s) or sound(s) it can represent. As with the previous lists, these should not be considered exhaustive but rather some examples to serve as a starting point.

Foreign Phonetics

German Consonants

German	English
b	b, p
ch	c (hard), k, ck
d	d, t
g	g, c (hard), k, ck
s	z
ss	s
sch	s (h)[4]
t	not equivalent to Eng. *d* but often used for it since Ger. hears no difference

---

[4] In words beginning with *s* followed by another consonant, Germans hear the *s* as *sh*. They sometimes add the *h* to English words even though the sound is not there in English.

German	English	German	English
h	often inserted after a vowel to emphasize that it is long	tsch	j
j	g (soft), y (consonant), ch	v	f, b
k	c (hard), k, ck	w	v
p	not equivalent to Eng. *b* but often used for it since Ger. hears no difference	z	ts, tz

German Vowels

German	English	German	English
a	short a, ah	ei	long i
aa	ah	ey	long i
ae	long a	eu	oi, oy
ai	long i	i	long e, short i
ay	long i	o	short o, oh
aeu	oi, oy	oo	long o
au	ou, ow	u	u
e	short e, long a	ue	short e, short i
ee	long a	y	i

French Consonants

French	English
c	s
ch	sh
g	j
ll	consonantal y
ng	ni of "senior"
oi (x)	wah
initial ou	w
qu	k

French Vowels

French	English
(e) au (x)	long o
e (s), e (z)	long a
i	long e

Spanish

Spanish	English
b	v (sound the same in Spanish)
v	b (sound the same in Spanish)
j	h
ll	consonantal y
es	Sp. adds *e* to words beginning in *s*, even though the sound is not there in English

Spanish	English
ndr	Sp. adds *d* between *n* and *r* even though the sound is not there in English
gu	initial *w*
final cons.	Sp. does not hear the second consonant of a final consonant pair; esp. when *d, t, b,* or *p*

Abbreviations

There is one additional factor that may lead to difficulties in interpreting inventories and that is common enough to deserve further treatment: the use of abbreviations and symbols. In modern usage, abbreviations generally fall into one of two categories. There are some standardized abbreviations for commonly used words (Mr., Dr., ea., pr., etc.), and non-standardized abbreviations usually made by leaving off the end of the word and replacing it with a period (abbrev., immed., etc.). Symbols are almost always standardized.

Forms of abbreviations used in inventories fall into only a few categories, but some of them do not fit into modern ideas of how words should be abbreviated. The end of the word may be omitted and the word followed by a period, a colon, or nothing at all. Middle sections of words are often left out and, although no apostrophe is used, the final letter of the word is sometimes added above the line. These superscripts are not usually familiar to modern readers. Here are some examples taken from Lord Botetort's inventory:

> 1 mahogy [mahogany] wine cooler
> 1 mahy [mahogany] ding [dining] table
> 2 Coppr [copper] coal scuttles
> 4 Staffordshe [Staffordshire] coffee pots
> 2 do [ditto] qt [quart] mugs
> 1 Deal box 1 diamd [diamond] stock buckle
> 1 pr [pair] of stone shoe & knee buckles
> 1 diad [diamond] Hatt buckle

It is noteworthy that within these few examples two words, mahogany and diamond, are each abbreviated two different ways. One cannot expect consistency even within the same inventory, much less between inventoriers. Three of the abbreviations used in the examples (for *ditto, pair,* and *quart)* are of the standardized type, and indeed, they survive unchanged even to today.

There are also some symbols used that are not found today. One of these is the use of *y* for *th.* Most people consider y^e to have been an archaic word for *the,* but the *y* should be considered a symbol rather than a letter, since it is used to represent the Old English letter *thorn,* which had a *th* sound. Thus ye was actually intended to be pronounced *the.* The same symbol is also found in forms such as y^{ere} (there), y^{is} (this), and y^t (that). Some other symbols still used today were used differently earlier. The symbol & is an example; today it is used strictly to mean and, but earlier its true meaning, *et* (Latin for *and*), was exploited more fully. Hence one finds it used as *&c* for *et cetera.* A more complete listing of some commonly encountered abbreviations and symbols appears at the end of the glossary in Chapter 4.

Some additional ideas for interpreting difficult words:

1) Whether or not a word is capitalized should not be given undue significance. It often means nothing.
2) There are some misspellings that defy analysis. It is often necessary to look for additional examples within the inventory to see whether the inventorier had his own personal usage for an oddly placed letter. For example, in one inventory an entry was found for a *hay faulk.* Other entries in the same inventory for *nifes* and *faulks* and a *flesh faulk* indicated that the word intended was *fork.* There is no rational basis for this odd spelling; it was simply a peculiarity of this inventorier.
3) Consider the context in which the word occurs. Although things are not always grouped logically, it can sometimes help. This is especially important if the unknown word occurs in a listing of debts, since it may be a proper name.
4) Consider the value of the object. Although it is important to realize that the relative worth of various items was not equivalent to today's, items such as adult animals did not have values of a few cents.

Example

The following inventory demonstrates many of the points made so far; indeed, it has a little of everything as far as problems are concerned. The handwriting is in general quite bad and the spelling is, to say the least, imaginative; to say the most, atrocious. It is the spelling that is really the matter of greatest interest. It is a hodgepodge of variants based on German phonetics, German accent, and English dialect. Occasionally all of these come into play simultaneously. The explanation which follows is given by line number; the line numbers were not present in the original but have been added for convenience.

	$	C
one Cow - - - - - - - - -	10	—
" Mare - - - - - - - -	5	—
a Sow and 4 Pigs - - - - -	10	—
a Do — 5 Do - - - - -	4	50
5 3 Hogs - - - - - - -	9	
Windmill - - - - - - -	2	—
a Shlay - - - - - - - -		75
a Iron Pot and a Teakettle & two Pans - -	1	25
4 Pails - - - - - - - -	1	
10 20 Do - - - - - - - -	5	—	4 350
a Lot of Tinware - - - - -	2	—
a Lot of Iron Ware - - - - -	1	—
2 Hightils - - - - - -	—	37½
a Lot of Wood Wair - - - - -	—	50
15 Flax and Tow yarn - - - - -	2	50
Pitchfork and Sheeds & Sundries - -	3	
5 Pieces of Linin Cloreght - - - -	8	
a Stove and Pipe - - - -	6	—
a Wool Weal and flax - - -	—	87½
20 a Reel - - - - - - -		37½
a Kitchintable - - - - - and Sundries	1		3 042½
4 Chirs - - - - - -	1	25
4 Do - - - - - -	—	75
a Tavil - - - - -	—	37½
25 a Bings - - - - -		25
a Chist and Sope and Sundries - - -	5	—
a Chist - - - - -	1	—
a Trunk and Sundries - - -	1	—
a Bivel & other Books - - - -	6	—
30 a Stilgert - - - - -	2	—
a Kittel & a Pot - - -		50
a Prase Kittel - - - -	5	—
a Chist and Sundries - - - -	1	—
a Spining Weal - - - -	—	50
35 a Lot of Iron - - - -	2	
	1	2 662½

Carlet - - - -	1	—
a Batetet and Bating - - - - -	2	—
a Baldet and Bating - - - - -	4	—
a do and do —	4	—
40	2 Stoner and Sundrae - -	2	—
40 Bushel of Rey - - -	15	—
15 Bushels of Weath - - -	12	75
a Tof and Stoner - - -	—	25
do do - - -	—	50
45	a Lot of old Eiron - - -	1	—
a Lot of old Euron & Sundreys - -	4	—
a Lot - - -		25
Body bison - - -	—	37 1/2
a Dole & Batetet - - -	6	—
50	a do do - - -	6	—

	$ 59 12 1/2

2 Safe Stener - - -	1	50
2 Siter Barel and Seider - -	1	—
	$ 2·50

In goods to - - -	$ 161·89 1/2
In Cash - - -	63 94	63 94
55	a Noth of Abraham Balef to - -	140 —	
Interest thereon to the 19th June 1828	6 30	146·30
	140 20	
a Noth of Jacob Stocher to	192 80	276·90
Interest thereon to the Day - -	84 10	
a Note of Jacob Shnyder to - - -	100 —	
60	Interest thereon - - -	3 10	103·10
a Note Andon Larch to - - -	90 00	
Interest thereon to - - -	27 55	117·55
a Note Andon Larch to - - -	50 —	
Interest thereon to - - -	18 12	68 12
a Bond Jacob Trase to - - -	460·00	489·12
65	Interest thereon - - -	29·12	
The Whole Appraisment amounts to $ 1492·10 1/2

Approved By us -
June the 19th 1828. Sworn
and Subscribed
before me - - -

George Brinker

Jacob R. Wimmer

Greorg Loof

~ 17 ~

Transliteration:

		$	¢	
	one Coww	10.00		
	a Mare	5.00		
	A Sow and 4 Peigs [pigs]	10.00		
	a Dito - 5 Doto	4.50		
5	3 Hougs [hogs]	9.00		
	Windmill	2.00		
	a Shlays [sleigh]	.75		
	a Eiran [iron] Pot and a Teakitel &			
	stove [?} Pans	1.25		
	4 Paks [bags]	1.00		
10	20 Baks [bags]	5.00		4350
	a Lot of Tenweir [tinwear]	2.00		
	a Lot of Eiron Ware	1.00		
	2 Highils [heckels]	.37	1/2	
	a Lot of Wooel Wair [wool wear]	.50		
15	Flaix [flax] and Toloyearn [tolo?yarn]	2.50		
	Plainkits [blankets] and Sheeds [sheets]			
	& Sunderes [sundries]	3.00		
	5 Peises [pieces] of Linin Clought			
	[linen cloth]	8.00		
	a Stove and Pipe	6.00		
	a Wool Woal [wheel] and flax	.37	1/2	
20	a Reeal [reel]	.37	1/2	
	a Kitzinbrasser [kitchen brasser] and			
	Suntres [sundries]	1.00		
	4 Chirs [chairs]	1.25		3042 1/2
	4 Dito	.75		
	a Tavil [table]	.37	1/2	
25	a Bings [benk?]	.37	1/2	
	a Chist [chest] and Sope [soap]			
	and Sundres	5.00		
	a Chist	1.00		
	a Traser [dresser] and Sundres	1.00		
	a Bivel [Bible] & other Books	6.00		
30	a Stilgert [stilgart]	2.00		
	a Kitel & a Pot	.50		
	a Prase [brass] Kitel	5.00		
	a Chist and Sundres	1.00		
	a Spining Weal [wheel]	.50		
35	a Lot of Eiron	2.00		
				2662 1/2
	Carbet [carpet]	1.00		
	a Batstet [bedstead] and Beting [bedding]	2.00		

	a Batstet and Beting	4.00	
	a Do and Dotto	4.00	
40	2 Staner [?] and Sundreas	2.00	
	40 Bushel of Rey [rye]	15.00	
	15 Bushels of Weath [wheat]	12.75	
	a Top [tub] and Stener [?]	.25	
	Doto and Dito	.50	
45	a Lot of old Eiron	1.00	
	a Lot of old Eiron & Sundrey	4.00	
	12 artin [?] Dits [?]	.25	
	Body Eiron	.37 1/2	
	a Bate [bed] & Batstet [bedstead]	6.00	
50	a Dot Do do	6.00	
			$59.12 1/2
	2 Sope [soap] Stener [?]	1.50	
	2 Siter Berels and Seider		
	[cider barrels and cider]	1.00	
			$ 2.50
	In goods to		$161.89 1/2
	In Cash	63.94	63.94
55	A Noth [Note] of Abraham Bapb to	140.00	146.30
	Interst thereon to the 19th June 1828	6.30	
	a Noth of Jacob Stocker to	192.80	276.90
	Interst thereon to this Day	84.10	
	a Note of Jacob Shnyder to	100.00	103.10
60	Interst thereon	3.10	
	a Note Andon Larch to	90.00	117.55
	Interes thereon to	27.55	
	a Note Andon Larch to	50.00	68.12
	Interst thereon to	18.12	
65	a Bond Jacob Frase to	460.00	489.12
	Interst thereon	29.12	
	the Whole Appraisment amounts to	$1492.10 1/2	

Explanations:

1. **Coww** [cow]: Although the third letter seems at first to be an *r*, making it such leaves the rest of the word unintelligible. Reading it as *w* leaves one with only a moderately misspelled cow, which fits the context nicely, both in terms of the following listings (also farm animals) and the valuation.

3. 4: The number is difficult to read, but it bears more resemblance to the 4 in line 4 than it does to the 9 in line 5 or the 8 in lines 17 and 64.

Peigs [peigs]: The final letter looks something like an *h*, but compare it to the *h's* in lines 8, 16, and 17. At the same time note the high stem on the final *s's in* lines 8 and 27. The use of the diphthong *ei* for short *i* is somewhat unusual, but considering the context, this must be the correct reading.

4. Dito, Doto [ditto, ditto]: Forms of this word are spelled almost every way but correctly throughout the inventory. It is also found abbreviated as *Do/do*. The uncrossed *t* appears frequently. It is also noteworthy that the t, uncrossed and with a spread-out stem, resembles a *t* in German script.

5. Hougs [hogs]: Again, the context makes it clear that the word is *hogs*. As in line 3, the use of a diphthong for a short vowel is unusual, but in this case it makes a little more sense as representing an (English) accent variation: the word is sometimes pronounced *howgs,* and *ou* can have an *ow* sound.

7. Schlays [sleighs]: *H*ere the accent variation is German. Germans pronounce words beginning in *sl* as if spelled *shl. Ay* and *eigh* both render the English long *a* sound; the writer simply chose the wrong one.

8. Eiran [iron]: This word is found elsewhere in the inventory, usually spelled *eiron.* This is an example of German phonetics, in which the English long *i i*s rendered as *ei.*

Kitel [kettle]: For the most part this is an English accent/dialect variant. The word is often pronounced just as spelled here, except that the *t* is usually doubled to make the *i* short. As pointed out earlier, consonants are often doubled or left single by caprice.

9. Paks [bags]: This could be read as *packs*, but the term was not frequently used at the time. It can be seen from lines 16 and 32 that the writer sometimes substitutes *p* for *b;* this is a German phonetic variant. The same phonetic system allows *k* to be substituted for final *g*. Reading the word as *bags* also fits with the valuation when compared to that of line 10: in each case one bag is worth 25¢.

10. Baks [bags]: Same explanation as line 9 except that the initial *b* has not been replaced by *p*.

11. Lot: *In* this context it means *a group r*ather than the more colloquial v*ery much.*

Tenweir [tinware]: The substitution of short *e* for short *i* is common. Although not very common, *ei c*an have a long *a s*ound in English.

13. Highils [heckles]: *T*he use of short *i* for short *e* (two places) is not uncommon. The *g* here has the *k s*ound of German phonetics (the reverse of the situation in lines 9 and 10). This is an example of a word that may give the modern reader difficulty in deciphering, since the word it is intended to represent is not common today. To figure out such words, it is often necessary to come up with as many spellings as possible and check each one in a dictionary or the glossary in Chapter 4.

14. Wooel [wool]: The writer apparently heard an extra syllable in the word.

Wair [wear]: The use of *ai f*or long *a*. Note that to this point this word (phonetically *ware = wear)* has been spelled *ware, weir,* and w*air.*

15. Flaix [flax]: Easy enough to decipher, but using *ai* for short *a* is unusual.

Toloyearn [tolo?yarn]: The yarn part is fairly easy to figure out, albeit unusually spelled. The *Tolo* part is more difficult—it doesn't seem to mean anything appropriate. If the top part of what appears to be an *l* is actually a random scribble, the word is *Tow,* which does not make sense.

16. Plainkits [blankets]: Use of *p* for *b* and short *i* for short *e* as mentioned earlier. Again, the unusual use of a diphthong (*ai*) for a short *a* sound; this seems to have been a personal peculiarity of this inventorier.

Sheeds [sheets]: The German phonetic use of *d* for *t*.

18. Woal [wheel]: This may actually be a simple matter of illegibility. The *o* may be an *e,* in which case one has the use of *ea* for long *e*.

19. Peises [pieces]: Interchanging *i* and *e* when used in combination is a problem that still plagues many. The use of *s* for soft *c* is common.

Clought [cloth]: German does not distinguish between final *t* and *th*, both have a *t* sound; hence, an accent variation.

20. Reeal [reel]: Another instance in which the writer apparently heard an extra syllable in the word.

21. Kitzinbrasser [kitchen brazier]: The use of *z* for a c*h* sound (rather than *sch)* is unusual even in German. The term *brasser f*or *brazier* is an English dialectic variant. Note also the use of long *s*.

22. Chirs [chairs]: Apparently a dialectic variant; it is found in many inventories written just this way.

24. Tavil [table]: The interchanging of *v* and *b* is not found in modern German; it is a characteristic of Pennsylvania Dutch. The word was deciphered by comparison to *Bivel i*n line 29, where the *v* must stand for a *b*.

25. Bings [benk?]: *T*his may be an attempt to render the Pennsylvania Dutch *benk* (final *g* standing for a *k* sound), meaning a type of bench.

28. Traser [dresser]: German phonetic substitution of *t* for *d*. Short *a* used for short *e* and use of a single rather than a double *s* are common.

29. Bivel [Bible]: That this is intended to mean *Bible* is indicated by the following phrase: *& other books*. See also note 24. *Le* is often written as *el*.

30. Stilgert [steelyard]: The problem here is more one of an unfamiliar word than of spelling; *steelgart* is a dialectic form of *steelyard*, a type of scale.

31. Prase [brass]: German phonetic use of *p* for *b*. Although modern rules of spelling would have the single *s* make the preceeding vowel long, here it remains short.

36. Carbet [carpet]: Again, the German phonetic substitution of *b* for *p*.

37. Betstet [bedstead]: Two examples of German phonetic use of *t* for *d*. The short *e* really comes closer to the sound in the word than the standard spelling with *ea*.

Beting [bedding]: Same substitution as in *Betstet,* but this time standing for double *d,* which is required by the addition of the suffix *-ing*.

39. Do [abbrev. ditto]: Although the *D* is very open, *t*his must be the correct reading, since another *ditto* follows and the valuation is the same as that of line 38.

40. Staner: The word is found two other places in this inventory (43 and 51, both spelled *stener)*. It is also found once in the inventory of the widow of the man whose goods are inventoried here (referred to there as *stenner)*. Among the Pennsylvania Germans, a word referring to a measuring scoop, usually, but not invariably, of tin.

41. Rey [rye]: German phonetic *ey* for long *i* sound.

42. Weath [wheat]: German final *th* used for *t (*see note 19b).

43. Top [tub]: German phonetic *p* for *b*. Substitution of short *o* for short *u*.

Stener: See note 40.

45. And: Note use of reflexed *d* here and in line 46.

47. 12: The number is a little difficult to read, primarily because of the use of a caret-shaped 1 (this is still common in Europe today).

Artin Dets [?]: This is another example of a "who knows?" The second word may well be a form of *ditto,* meaning more "old iron" is being listed. In this case the first word must be a qualifying adjective or a type of container or unit of measure, but all variations tried failed to yield the solution. *Artin* may be an attempt to render *earthen*.

48. Body: Here the word probably means "a group of," rather than "for the body." Armor is rarely mentioned in inventories as late as this one.

50. **Dodo** [abbrev. ditto]: Two ditto abbreviations, one for each syllable above.

51. **Stener**: *S*ee note 40.

52. **Siter/Seider** [both cider]: Both words are the same, but are spelled differently. *S* *i*s often used for soft *c* (which German does not have). The interchangeabilityof *d* and *t* is again demonstrated. The *ei* in the second word is a German phonetic for long *i*.

54. **In:** Note that the capital *I* looks more like a *J*. The writer's capital *J* (line 57) looks more like an *I*.

55. **Noth** [note]: *Th* for *t* (see note 19b).

    Babp: Another substitution of *p* for *b*. This man's name is usually spelled Babb, although this misspelling does give a clue as to how the name was pronounced at the time.

61. **Andon Larch:** The name should be Anton Lerch, but again, this gives a clue as to how the name was pronounced.

CHAPTER 2

HOW MUCH IS THAT WORTH?

Anyone who has traveled in a foreign country has probably encountered this scenario: An American is involved in a discussion with a salesperson in some store. When the clerk, upon being queried, gives the price of the item in question, the potential customer replies, "Yes, but how much is that in *real* money?" Along the same line, I recall that during my first trip to Canada, a cousin of mine confided to me that he had to be careful when making a purchase in Canadian currency. "It's like using Monopoly money," he explained. "It doesn't seem like you're spending the real thing, so it's easy to spend too much." What these examples point out is that it is difficult to comprehend the value of a sum of money when it is given in an unfamiliar frame of reference.

This problem is common to almost all inventories. Earlier documents have values given in unfamiliar currencies, and sometimes even in terms of commodities. Even later inventories in which the values are given in dollars presents difficulties, because the relative value of the dollar has changed over the years. Although it may not seem to be the case at first glance, all the modes of valuation mentioned above share the same basic problem: they are all matters of relative rather than absolute value.

Whether one realizes it or not, the reason he must convert foreign currency to "real money" before he can grasp the cost involved, is that he must bring the amount into his normal frame of reference for evaluation. Once he has arrived back on his home ground, he can apply the usual, albeit generally subconscious, method of determining the relative cost. He compares. In some cases it is a matter of comparison with costs involved in his day-to-day life—how many loaves of bread could he buy for that amount; how many rent payments is that, etc.? In other cases, the comparison is to his income—how many hours would he have to work to make that much? Both methods are quite valid, and when one is dealing

TABLE I

Prices[1] of Chesapeake & Maryland Tobacco: 1618 - 1775[2]

Year	Price	Year	Price	Year	Price	Year	Price	Year	Price	Year	Price	Year	Price
1618	27.00	1641	---	1664	1.35	1687	0.85	1710	0.85	1733	0.84	1756	1.07
1619	27.00	1642	4.20	1665	1.10	1688	0.75	1711	0.97	1734	0.97	1757	1.16
1620	12.00	1643	1.80	1666	0.90	1689	0.70	1712	1.00	1735	0.93	1758	1.29
1621	20.00	1644	2.55	1667	1.10	1690	0.80	1713	1.00	1736	1.02	1759	2.05
1622	18.00	1645	1.50	1668	1.25	1691	0.80	1714	0.71	1737	0.93	1760	1.60
1623	16.00	1646	2.20	1669	1.15	1692	0.80	1715	0.72	1738	1.02	1761	1.54
1624	13.00	1647	2.00	1670	1.15	1693	0.75	1716	0.80	1739	1.01	1762	1.39
1625	---[3]	1648	1.50	1671	1.05	1694	0.75	1717	0.79	1740	0.80	1763	1.10
1626	---	1649	3.00	1672	1.00	1695	0.75	1718	0.89	1741	0.62	1764	1.26
1627	---	1650	---	1673	1.00	1696	0.85	1719	1.04	1742	0.67	1765	1.33
1628	---	1651	---	1674	1.00	1697	0.90	1720	1.19	7143	0.67	1766	1.45
1629	---	1652	---	1675	1.00	1698	1.00	1721	0.97	1744	0.63	1767	1.63
1630	---	1653	2.60	1676	1.05	1699	1.05	1722	0.86	1745	0.56	1768	1.81
1631	4.00	1654	2.80	1677	1.15	1700	1.00	1723	1.07	1746	0.61	1769	2.23
1632	3.4	1655	2.00	1678	1.05	1701	0.95	1724	0.90	1747	0.45	1770	2.06
1633	5.00	1656	2.25	1679	1.05	1702	1.00	1725	1.05	1748	0.67	1771	1.90
1634	---	1657	2.00	1680	1.00	1703	0.85	1726	0.91	1749	0.76	1772	1.54
1635	5.00	1658	2.10	1681	0.90	1704	0.90	1727	0.82	1750	1.16	1773	1.48
1636	5.35	1659	1.65	1682	0.80	1705	0.80	1728	0.67	1751	1.16	1774	1.41
1637	3.00	1660	1.50	1683	0.80	1706	0.80	1729	0.70	1752	1.48	1775	1.67
1638	3.00	1661	1.50	1684	0.80	1707	0.90	1730	0.67	1753	1.16		
1639	3.00	1662	1.60	1685	1.00	1708	0.90	1731	0.65	1754	1.04		
1640	2.50	1663	1.55	1686	1.00	1709	0.90	1732	0.74	1755	0.85		

1. Prices are given in pence sterling per pound of tobacco.
2. Prices for 1618 - 1658 are for Chesapeake tobacco; the rest are for Maryland tobacco.
3. Indicates that no price was available for that year.

with inventoried values, it is essential to make the same kinds of comparisons.

Before one can make these comparisons, he must have a means of putting himself into the frame of reference that existed at the time, or of converting the amounts into equivalents that fit his own frame of reference. Hopefully, the following sections will provide sufficient data for accomplishing this. Since comprehension of this data requires some knowledge of the currencies in use at the time, this matter will also be covered.

Currencies

From the first moment this continent was settled by Europeans there have been problems with currency, a fact usually attributable to the lack of it. This is not to say that there was necessarily a lack of wealth; it was hard cash, for use as a medium of exchange, that was in short supply. The first adaptation to this situation was the use of so-called "commodity money." This was basically a form of barter, but eventually certain commodities became the standard media of exchange for such purposes as paying taxes. In early New England, first grains and then beaver pelts were used, while in southern areas such as Virginia and Maryland, tobacco served the purpose. This system was unwieldy for domestic applications and totally worthless for international ones. What was needed was legal tender.

With the exception of tobacco in the South, commodity money need not concern anyone studying estate inventories. New England and the central colonies abandoned it fairly early. At least in Virginia, however, inventoried values continued to be given in terms of pounds of tobacco through most of the seventeenth century. Table 1[5] gives the prices for tobacco over a span of years to aid those who must deal with such valuations.

Even though central and northern parts of America soon did away with the use of commodity money, other problems were waiting to fill the gap. The people were obliged to use whatever kind of money was available, and this led to the simultaneous use of a conglomeration of foreign (i.e. non-British and later non-United States) money. Early account books show that merchants received payment in a variety of coins, all of which had to be reduced to their equivalents in British money. Not every kind of foreign currency was used in every part of the country, and the types which predominated depended on the area in question.

---

[5] Table 1 taken from U.S. Bureau of the Census, *Historical Statistics of the United States to 1970*, Bicentennial ed., Pt. 1 (Washington, D.C.: 1975).

Some of the foreign gold coins in circulation were the French guinea and pistole, the Portuguese moidore and johannes or "joe," and the Spanish doubloon and pistole. Foreign silver coins included French crowns and livres, and Spanish dollars and "pieces" (parts of pieces of eight).[6] Of all these, the Spanish milled dollar (also called a piece of eight, a piastre, and a peso duro) was by far the most common and indeed, was virtually ubiquitous. Its popularity was primarily due to its availability. Its use had become so widespread that it was later used as the basis for the currency of the United States, and it continued to be legal tender until 1857 (valued at par with the U. S. dollar). Although the researcher is not likely to have to deal with values given in terms of these foreign currencies (except the Spanish dollar), unless he is dealing with personal account books, he may occasionally encounter them in inventories in listings of "cash on hand." All these coins are included in the glossary in Chapter 3.

Although these various currencies were used as the actual media of exchange, valuations were almost always given in terms of pounds/shillings/pence, or dollars (either Spanish or U. S.). Consequently, if the researcher is familiar with these systems, he should be able to deal with most inventories handily. The problem with them lies in the fact that with the exception of the U. S. dollar, none of these currency systems are decimal.

Since it is often necessary to be able to do calculations in these currency systems (e.g. to verify an unclear number), one must understand them. In the pounds/shillings/pence system (abbreviated £/s/d)[7] the basic unit is the pound. Each pound is made up of twenty shillings, each of which is made up of twelve pence. In the Spanish system the basic unit is the dollar, each of which is made up of eight reales (also called esculins). Some examples of arithmetic using these systems should clarify them. Note that in most cases the only real problem is that of simplifying the result of converting from one subunit of the currency to another. The latter is necessary in subtraction, when one must "borrow," and in division, when one "carries over" or converts everything to the lowest subunit (pence or reales).

---

[6] MS Reports, Committee on Finance, Continental Congress, Vol. 26; reprinted in International Monetary Conference, 1878, p. 422; as reported in A. Barton Hepburn, *A History of Currency in the United States* (New York: MacMillan Co., 1915).

[7] The symbol used to separate the subunits of this currency varies. The most common are: / (used here), :, and -. Double decimal points (..) are also used occasionally; they were used also for the Spanish dollar and reales in the only examples encountered.

1. Addition

a) £/s/d: 1/16/5
              18/6
    + 5/19/9
        6/53/20

b) $..reales: 8..4
             15..7
         + 0..7
         23..18

In each of these examples the raw total is achieved simply by adding up the subunits. The results must still be simplified. In a): 20 pence is equivalent to 1 shilling/8 pence (there is one 12 in 20 with 8 left over). The total has now become 6/54/8. Since 54 shillings is equivalent to 2 pounds/14 shillings (there are two 20's in 54 with 14 left over), the total can now be expressed as 8/14/8.

By similar reasoning (albeit with different units) b) can be simplified by noting that 18 reales is equivalent to 2 dollars ..2 reales (there are two 8's in 18 with 2 left over). The total can now be written as $25..2.

2. Multiplication

a) £/s/d: 1/5/4
          x 5
      5/25/20

b) $ ..reales 8..4
        x 10
     80..40

Multiplication is accomplished basically just as addition. The subunits are multiplied separately and the resulting product simplified. In a) it is noted that 20 pence is equivalent to 1 shilling/8 pence; the product has now become 5/26/8. Since the 26 shillings is equivalent to 1 pound/6 shillings, the product may be further simplified to 6/6/8.

Example b) is also a matter of simplification of the raw product. Since the 40 reales is equivalent to 5 dollars, the product may be restated at $85..0.

3. Subtraction

a) £/s/d: 6/ 2/5
        - 1/12/7

The usual procedure would be to simply subtract each subunit separately and simplify the result. In this case, the subtraction cannot take place as the numbers stand. As with regular subtraction, one must borrow. But remember that you are not borrowing 10's, 100's, etc. but 12's and 20's. Borrowing 1 shilling in the form of 12 pence from the 2 shillings changes the upper number to:

6/ 1/17
- 1/12/ 7

~ 29 ~

This solves the problem with the pence, which can now be subtracted. The shillings column still needs work. Borrowing 1 pound in the form of 20 shillings changes the problem to:

$$
\begin{array}{r}
5/21/17 \\
- \quad 1/12/\ 7 \\
\hline
4/\ 9/10
\end{array}
$$

If necessary, the answer would be simplified.

b) $ ..reales 8..4
                    - 5..6

As in the example above, some borrowing must be done. One dollar in the form of 8 reales is borrowed from the 8 dollars. The problem now becomes:

$$
\begin{array}{r}
7..12 \\
- \quad 5..\ 6 \\
\hline
2..\ 6
\end{array}
$$

4. Division:

There are two types of division one may have to perform. In the first case the monetary amount is divided by a simple number; in the second type a monetary amount is divided by another monetary amount. The first type can be approached in two ways, the second of which is the same as the method used for the second type of division. To keep things as simple as possible, only the method common to both types will be discussed here. The method requires that all monetary amounts be expressed in terms of the lowest subunit (pence or reales) alone. Standard division is then performed and the quotient is simplified.

a) £/s/d: 4 | 1/2/4

Converting the 1/2/4 to pence is basically the reverse of simplification. The 1 pound is equivalent to 20 shillings, making the amount 22/4. The 22 shillings is equivalent to 22 x 12 = 264 pence. Adding the remaining 4 pence onto this gives 268 pence. The problem now can be expressed as:

$$
\begin{array}{r}
67 \\
4\ |\ \overline{268} \\
- 24 \\
\hline
28 \\
- 28 \\
\hline
\end{array}
$$

The quotient, 67 pence, must now be simplified. Sixty-seven pence is equivalent to 5 shillings/7 pence (there are 5 12's in 67 with 7 left over). Five/seven cannot be simplified any further, but had the number of shillings exceeded 20, additional simplification to express the even multiples of 20 as pounds would have been necessary.

b) £/s/d: $13/3 \overline{\smash{\big)}\ 2/1/10}$

The first step is to express both the divisor and the dividend in terms of pence alone. The 13 shillings is equivalent to 13 x 12 = 156 pence. Adding on the 3 pence gives a result of 159 pence. In the other number the 2 pounds is equivalent to 2 x 20 = 40 shillings. This makes the number 41/10, which must still be reduced to pence. The 41 shillings is equivalent to 41 x 12 = 492 pence. Adding on the final 10 pence yields 502 pence. The division can now be done.

$$
\begin{array}{r}
3.15 + 125/159 \text{ approx.} = 3.16 \\
159 \overline{\smash{\big)}\ 502.00} \\
\underline{477} \\
250 \\
\underline{159} \\
910 \\
\underline{795} \\
125
\end{array}
$$

This result, which is not a monetary amount, does not need simplification.

c) $..reales: $4 \overline{\smash{\big)}\ 8..4}$

Converting 8 dollars and 4 reales to reales, we get 8 x 8 = 64 + 4 or 68 reales. The problem has now become:

$$
\begin{array}{r}
17 \\
4 \overline{\smash{\big)}\ 68} \\
\underline{4} \\
28 \\
\underline{28}
\end{array}
$$

This result is in reales and must be simplified. Seventeen reales is equivalent to 2 dollars and 1 real, 2..1, which is the final result.

d) $ ..reales: $4..2 \overline{\smash{\big)}\ 22..0}$

As in example b), the first step is to express everything as reales. The 4..2 is equivalent to 4 x 8 + 2 = 32 reales. The other number is equivalent to 22 x 8 + 0 = 176 reales. We may now divide.

$$
\begin{array}{r}
5.5 \\
32\,|\overline{\,176.0} \\
\underline{160} \\
160 \\
\underline{160}
\end{array}
$$

This result is not monetary and does not need simplification.

Colonial and State Currencies

Many people wonder why some inventories made after the Revolutionary War and after the establishment of the U. S. currency system were still giving values in terms of pounds/shillings/pence. They were not being valued in terms of pounds sterling (the British currency) but rather in "current money of the state." When still colonies, these states had

TABLE 2

Exchange Rate[1] for Colonial Currency vs. Pound Sterling

Colony	1701	1708	1774
New England	137	155	133
New York	155	155	179
Eastern New Jersey	155	---[2]	170
Western New Jersey	181	---	170
Pennsylvania	181	178	170[3]
South Carolina	161	161	700
North Carolina	---	---	177
Virginia	111	120	132
Maryland	---	133	167

1. Rate represents the number of pounds in colonial currency equivalent to 100 pounds sterling.
2. Indicates data not available.
3. For Pennsylvania see also Table 3.

TABLE 3
Exchange Rate[1] for Pennsylvania Currency
vs. Pound Sterling

Year	Rate	Year	Rate	Year	Rate	Year	Rate	Year	Rate	Year	Rate
1720	133.33	1730	151.69	1740	164.06	1750	171.10	1760	160.30	1770	153.99
1721	133.33	1731	153.13	1741	145.18	1751	170.63	1761	174.12	1771	165.57
1722	133.33	1732	161.10	1742	159.69	1752	166.66	1762	175.84	1772	161.21
1723	---[2]	1733	165.00	1743	160.31	1753	167.96	1763	173.13	1773	165.80
1724	---	1734	---	1744	167.35	1754	168.15	1764	172.38	1774	169.74
1725	---	1735	162.50	1745	175.70	1755	168.88	1765	171.58	1775	166.04
1726	---	1736	165.13	1746	179.25	1756	172.52	1766	165.35		
1727	150.00	1737	167.50	1747	184.56	1757	165.96	1767	166.20		
1728	150.00	1738	167.50	1748	174.33	1758	159.21	1768	166.36		
1729	150.00	1739	170.00	1749	172.36	1759	154.71	1769	158.31		

1. Rate represents the number of pounds of local currency equivalent to 100 pounds sterling.
2. Indicates data not available.

issued money and they had naturally used the system with which everyone was familiar at the time. Under the Constitution, each state was permitted to issue its own currency. The federal government merely retained the right to regulate its value relative to the currencies of the other states. The currencies issued when the states had been colonies continued to be used.

What one is less likely to realize simply by reading inventories from before the War for Independence is that the same situation applied as far as colonial inventories were concerned. They are not usually in pounds sterling but in "current money of the colony." Although state currencies were (at least supposedly) at par with one another, the same was certainly not true of the currencies of the various colonies. The researcher must keep this in mind when dealing with money matters before the break with England.

Tables 2 and 3[8] give some of the values of colonial currency with reference to the pound sterling. While converting colonial currency to pounds sterling does little good in its own right, these tables give one the means of evaluating the currency of one colony with respect to that of another. This is important when trying to establish a frame of reference

---

[8] Table 2 consists of data taken passim from A. Barton Hepburn, *A History of Currency in the United States* (New York: MacMillan Co., 1915); and Alice Hanson Jones, *American Colonial Wealth*, Vol. 3 (New York: Arno Press, 1977). Table 3 is from U. S. Bureau of the Census, *Historical Statistics of the United States, Colonial Times to 1970*, Pt. 1 (Washington, D.C.: 1975).

(see next section). It does little good, for example, to evaluate an inventory from Maryland in terms of labor rates from Pennsylvania without taking into account the fact that the two are given in terms of different currencies. Note that all tables in this chapter (unless otherwise noted) are given in terms of local currency.

Frames of Reference

While I was in the library researching some matter for this book, I couldn't help but overhear a conversation between two high school students who were going through some microfilms of old newspapers, probably for some school project. They were absolutely amazed by the prices of various foodstuffs in the advertisements. The problem, of course, although they didn't realize it, was that they were evaluating these prices in terms of their own frame of reference rather than in terms of that existing at the time the newspapers were printed. The same problem is always encountered when one attempts to evaluate the relative worth of items in inventories. You must put yourself into the frame of reference that existed at the time the inventory was made, or convert the values into current dollars so that your own frame of reference can be used.

For inventories made after 1800, it is possible to convert the amounts given into current dollars by using consumer price indices. These indices give the relative buying power of the dollar with reference to dollar values for a given year (the reference year) over a span of time. Table 4[9] contains factors calculated from consumer price indices that allow you to convert a dollar amount for any year between 1800 and 1900 into the equivalent amount of 1982 dollars. To convert an amount, simply multiply it by the factor given for the year in which the inventory was made. See examples at the end of this chapter.

Since there is a paucity of consumer price index data available for the period before 1800, other methods must be employed. As has been mentioned earlier, there are two basic ways in which people evaluate how large a sum of money is—they compare it to the costs of other items, or consider it in terms of labor required to earn that sum. Of these two, the "labor required" method probably would have the most meaning to the greatest number of people. Unfortunately, continuous data on wage rates

---

[9] Table 4 is based on data from U. S. Bureau of the Census, *Historical Statistics of the United States, Colonial Times to 1970*, Series E 135-166. Update to 1982 based on CPI's from U. S. Bureau of the Census data for 1982 (based on the same reference year, 1967).

TABLE 4

Factors for Converting to 1982 Dollars

Year	Fctr.	Year	Fctr.	Year	Fctr.	Year	Fctr.	Year	Fctr.	Year	Fctr.
1774[1]	80.48	1816	5.63	1833	9.90	1850	11.48	1867	6.84	1884	10.63
1800	5.63	1817	5.98	1834	9.57	1851	11.48	1868	7.18	1885	10.63
1801	5.74	1818	6.24	1835	9.26	1852	11.48	1869	7.18	1886	10.63
1802	6.68	1819	6.24	1836	8.70	1853	11.48	1870	7.56	1887	10.63
1803	6.38	1820	6.83	1837	8.44	1854	10.63	1871	7.98	1888	10.63
1804	6.38	1821	7.18	1838	9.57	1855	10.25	1872	7.98	1889	10.63
1805	6.38	1822	7.18	1839	9.57	1856	10.63	1873	7.98	1890	10.63
1806	6.11	1823	7.98	1840	9.57	1857	10.25	1874	8.44	1891	10.63
1807	6.53	1824	8.70	1841	9.26	1858	11.04	1875	8.70	1892	10.63
1808	5.98	1825	8.44	1842	9.90	1859	10.63	1876	8.97	1893	10.63
1809	6.11	1826	8.44	1843	10.25	1860	10.63	1877	8.97	1894	11.04
1810	6.11	1827	8.44	1844	10.25	1861	10.63	1878	9.90	1895	11.48
1811	5.74	1828	8.70	1845	10.25	1862	9.57	1879	10.25	1896	11.48
1812	5.63	1829	8.97	1846	10.63	1863	9.57	1880	9.90	1897	11.48
1813	4.95	1830	8.97	1847	10.25	1864	6.11	1881	9.90	1898	11.48
1814	4.56	1831	8.97	1848	11.04	1865	6.24	1882	9.90	1899	11.48
1815	5.22	1832	9.57	1849	11.48	1866	6.53	1883	10.25	1900	11.48

1. Factor for 1774 converts pounds sterling to 1982 dollars.

in a given area over a long span of time are difficult to come by. A few for various parts of the country during different time periods are given in Tables 5-8,[10] but the listings are so scattered with respect to time and place that consistent application of this method would be difficult at best. Prices of various commodities, on the other hand, are available. Tables 9-12[11] give the **wholesale** prices of flour and sugar for four cities for the period up to 1800. One can therefore apply the "comparison of costs" method more generally, but this method also has some serious problems built into it. These are discussed in more detail below.

Application of either of the two methods mentioned above is not especially difficult, but some current data must be supplied by the researcher. One must have some idea of the current average wages for skilled and unskilled labor. One can, of course, supply this data from his own experience. For example, if it is determined that the value of a certain inventory

---

[10] Tables 5-7 taken from U. S. Bureau of the Census, *Historical Statistics of the United States, Colonial Times to 1970*, Bicentennial Ed., Part 1 (Washington, D. C.: 1975). Table 8 modified from Richard Walsh, *Charleston's Sons of Liberty* (Columbia, S.C.: Univ. of South Carolina Press, 1959).

[11] Raw data for Tables 9-12 from Arthur Harrison Cole, *Wholesale Commodity Prices in the United States 1700-1861, Statistical Supplement* (Cambridge, Mass.: Harvard Univ. Press, 1938). Some data incorporated into Table 9 from Anne Bezanson, et al., *Wholesale Prices in Philadelphia 1784-1861* (Philadelphia, Pa.: Univ. of Pennsylvania Press, 1936).

was equivalent to two-and-one-half year's labor, and you are currently making $20,000 per year, the value is roughly equivalent to $50,000. It must also be taken into account, however, that your take-home pay is not, in fact, $20,000 but probably closer to $15,000. Current wages are subject to many taxes and other types of withholding that did not apply when the inventory was made. The value of $37,500 current money is probably closer in terms of buying power. It should also be noted that not everyone is making $20,000 per year; some make more, others less. Consequently, although converting the inventory value to current dollars based on your own salary may speak meaningfully to you, it will not do so for others. One should therefore rely on average wages to supply the basis for comparison. In the final analysis, the best way to apply this method is to leave the value in terms of the amount of labor required at the time to earn that amount of money. This will have meaning for anyone.

When using the "comparison of costs" method, one must keep a couple of things in mind. First of all, note that the tables given here deal with wholesale prices; they must therefore be compared to current wholesale prices, not to retail prices. Secondly, one must remember that the relative cost of food has changed over the years in a direction that one would not at first think possible—it has gotten cheaper. While it must be granted that the wholesale price has increased, it has not, in fact, increased to the extent that it should have if inflation were the only factor.

Raw sugar today costs only about twice what it cost 150 years ago (on a wholesale, dollar-for-dollar basis). This, when considered in a vacuum, would imply that yesterday's dollar had only about twice the buying power of today's. A glance at Table 4 will tell you that that is not the case. The difference lies primarily in the fact that food today is cheaper in terms of the percentage of the average family's income its purchase requires. It is therefore cheaper in terms of labor required to purchase it. Ten dollars spent on food in 1800 may well have represented one-half of a family's monthly income; the same ten dollars today probably represents no more than one-fiftieth.

Although data on the percentage of family income spent on food during the seventeenth and eighteenth centuries is as difficult to find as wage rates, the following may help: "[In eighteenth-century Boston] the typical urban family spent up to 50 percent of its income on food. . . . Today [1980], the average American family spends about seventeen percent of its after-tax income on groceries. . . ."[12] This implies that a given amount of money in the 1700's had about one-third of the food-

[12] Edwin J. erkins, Edwin J. *The Economy of Colonial America* (New York: Columbia Univ. Press, 1980).

buying power as the same amount today. In terms of labor involved in the purchase of a month's groceries, today's worker need work only one-third as long as someone in the 1700's. For this reason, when using the comparison of costs method based on food prices, it would be a good idea to at least triple the inventoried amount before converting the money into commodities for further conversion into current dollars.

Application of either of the two methods mentioned above is not difficult, but some current data must be supplied by the researcher. One must have some idea of the current average wages in the country or of the average wholesale prices of commodities. Either of these should be available in the reference department of any public library; they are usually to be found in publications of the U. S. Government. The specifics of applying these methods are best described by example, and several such examples are to be found at the end of this chapter.

There is one additional device that can be employed in evaluating the relative value of inventories. It has not been mentioned up to this point, since it is very labor-intensive and yields basically only qualitative results. Like the other methods, it is a form of comparison, but unlike the other methods one must generate the reference data himself. It consists of comparing the value of the inventory in which you have interest to the average values of other inventories made in the same area at about the same time.

All one need do is go through the inventories for the same year and average all the net values. How much work this entails is a function of the area and the time period. However, for the comparison to be of any value the data base must be large enough to insure that a general cross-section of the population is being sampled (at least 100 inventories). What one ends up with is a basis for stating that the inventory in question reflects wealth that was less than, about the same as, or more than the average for the area at the time. This method shares one advantage with the labor required method. It is not subject to constant fluctuations in the economy. It seems unlikely that in a hundred years values in 1982 dollars will have much more meaning to the average reader than values in 1880 dollars would have to a reader today.

Some final comments need to be made with regard to evaluating the net wealth of the person whose inventory is being studied. First of all, one must wonder how accurate the appraised values are. Most people are aware, for example, that the appraised value of real estate for tax purposes is usually quite a bit below the actual market value of that property. This seems not to have been the case with inventories in general. Of early English inventories, Ashmore states, ". . . and while there is always a tendency to undervalue for probate, my own experience does not suggest any wide gap between current [i.e. at that time] prices and those recorded by the 'praisers.'"[13] After studying inventories through America in 1774, Jones noted that there was a ". . . close correspondence between appraised values and the sums realized by actual sale of assets for the same estate."[14]

One must also question the completeness of the inventories. Jones mentions that items were occasionally listed among items sold at auction that never appeared in the appraisal.[15] She also notes, and this is of extreme importance, that "only in New England were land and buildings, that is 'real estate,' regularly listed and valued in the probate inventories of 1774. In all other regions, I found listed only 'personal estate,' that is moveables, rights and credits. . . . Exceptions occurred in nine cases in Northampton County, Pennsylvania, where, in addition to 'personal estate' items, land entries were made and valued, then crossed out, but in such a way that they are still legible. Land information also appeared on two New York inventories and one or two in Philadelphia."[16]

The reader should note that in the sample inventory given in Chapter 1 there is no mention of land or buildings, even though deed records indicate that the deceased had land holdings. The effect that this omission would have with respect to the inventoried value's telling you something about the net worth of an individual can be estimated by asking yourself

TABLE 5
Average Daily Wage Rates of Artisans and Laborers[1]
Philadelphia Area

Year	Artisans	Laborers	Year	Artisans	Laborers	Year	Artisans	Laborers
1785	$1.33	$0.70	1790	$1.01	$0.50	1795	$1.66	$1.00
1786	1.00	---	1791	1.05	0.53	1796	1.74	1.00
1787	1.00	0.53	1792	1.00	0.66	1797	1.83	1.00
1788	0.97	---	1793	1.25	0.80	1798	1.57	1.00
1789	1.00	0.52	1794	1.39	1.00	1799	1.62	1.00

1. Non-agricultural laborers; wages for agricultural laborers average about one-half the amounts stated here.

---

[13] Owen Ashmore, "Inventories as a Source of Local History 1—Houses" (*The Amateur Historian*, Vol. 4 (1958-59), p. 157.
[14] Alice Hanson Jones, *American Colonial Wealth*, 2nd ed., Vol. 1 (New York: Arno Press, 1977) p. 15.
[15] Ibid., p. 16.
[16] Ibid.

TABLE 6
Daily Wages of Selected Types of Workmen, by Area

Area and Year	Wages [pounds/shillings/pence][1]					
	Carpenters	Masons and Bricklayers	Joiners and Riggers	Coopers	Tailors	Laborers
Virginia, 1621	4/0	4/0	5/0	4/0	3/0	3/0
Massachusetts, 1633	2/0	2/0	2/0	---	---	1/6
New Haven, 1640	2/6	2/6	2/6	2/6	---	2/0
New Haven, 1641	2/0	2/0	2/0	2/0	---	1/6
Massachusetts, 1670	2/0	2/0	---	2/8[3]	1/8	1/3 to 2/0
South Carolina, 1710	3/0 to 5/0	6/0	3/0 to 5/0	4/0	5/0	---
Rhode Island, 1776	5/0	6/6	5/0	5/0	---	3/0
Providence, 1779	3/12/0	3/13/0	3/12/0	---	17/0/0[2]	2/8/0
Virginia, 1781	6/0	5/0	---	5/0	5/0	2/0

1. Amounts in local currency.
2. Per suit.
3. For a 32 gal. barrel.

how much of your own "worth" is tied up in real estate. For most people, their house constitutes a very large portion of their net worth.

Even after real estate has been taken into account, many inventories still reflect very meager wealth. Perkins makes some comments on standards of living that are equally of significance here: "The accepted view of what level of income constitutes wealth or poverty in America has changed over time. Colonial incomes, high by the standards of the time, were about fifty percent lower than the official poverty line established by the U. S. Government for a farm family of five members in 1979. . . . Poverty and wealth, beyond a minimal subsistence figure of perhaps $300 a year, have become relative concepts over time and between cultures."[17]

It must be remembered that during the early years of this country, most of the people were involved in agriculture and practiced a subsistence lifestyle. They took care of their own basic needs and did not generate much extra income. Those inventories that list even modest amounts of possessions often reflect a very high standard of living, since they often constitute a listing of luxuries. Many items we would consider basics, such as stoves, were, in fact, not necessities; they could just as well have cooked food in the fireplace.

---

[17] Edwin J. Perkins, *The Economy of Colonial America* (New York: Columbia Univ. Press, 1980), p. 148.

TABLE 7
Daily and Monthly Wages[1] of Agricultural Laborers in Maryland

Year	Daily	Monthly	Year	Daily	Monthly	Year	Daily	Monthly	Year	Daily	Monthly
1638	---	8/4	1647	2/6	21/3	1655[2]	3/9	---	1669[2]	2/6	24/10
1641	2/0	---	1648	2/6	41/8	1656	2/6	---	1670	---	21/10
1642	0/9	5/0	1649	2/6	---	1660[2]	---	18/9	1676	---	25/0
1644[2]	1/3	20/3	1652	---	100/0	1662	---	26/8			
1645	---	21/3	1654	---	100/0	1667	---	25/0			

1. Rates in shill./pence sterling   2. Avg. of 2 (or 3) rates available that year.

TABLE 8
Daily Wages, Charleston, SC

Year	Occupation	Wages[1]	Year	Occupation	Wages[1]
1710	Tailors	5/0	1766	Wheelwrights	1/10/0 plus
1710	Shoemakers	2/6			4/0 rations
1710	Smiths	7/6	1766	Shinglemakers	7/6 plus
1710	Weavers	3/0			4/0 rations
1710	Bricklayers	6/0	1766	Clerks	6/8
1710	Coopers	4/0	1766	Laborers	7/6 plus
1710	Carpenters	3/0 to 5/0			4/0 rations
1710	Joiners	3/0 to 5/0	1767	Negro Carpenters	1/0/0
1710	Laborers	1/3 to 2/0 plus	1768	Saddlers	1/0/0
		diet & lodging	1770	Coopers	1/10/0
1740	Master Carpenters	2/0/0	1771	Cabinet-makers,	35/0/0 per month
1740	Master Joiners	2/0/0		Employees	
1740	Negro Carpenters	1/5/0	1772	Cabinet-makers,	36/0/0 per month
1740	Carpenters, Appren-			Employees	
	tices, White & Black		1773	Journeyman Carpen-	1/7/4
	1st Year	7/6		ters	
	2nd Year	10/0	1773	Master Carpenters	2/15/0
	3rd Year	15/0	1775	Carpenters	15/0 to 45/0 plus
	4th Year	1/0/0			1 gill rum
1740	Bricklayers	2/0/0	1778	Negro Laborers	1/0/0 and compensa-
1760	Wheelwrights	1/1/4 plus			tion if hurt
		4/0 rations	1781	Ship-carpenters	13/6 sterling
1760	Blacksmiths	3/0/0 plus	1782	Negro Carpenters	3/6 sterling
		4/0 rations	1783	Journeyman Carpen-	2/9/0
1760	Wheelwrights	1/15/0 plus		ters	
		4/0 rations	1783	Master Carpenters	3/5/0
1766	Carpenters	1/10/0 plus	1783	Master Carpenters	4/17/6
		4/0 rations			(rumored)
1766	Blacksmiths	1/0/0 plus			
		4/0 rations			

1. Wages in pounds/shillings/pence local currency unless otherwise noted.

TABLE 9
Average Annual Wholesale Prices
Philadelphia

Year	Flour s/cwt[1]	Sugar s/cwt	Year	Flour s/cwt	Sugar s/cwt	Year	Flour s/cwt	Sugar s/cwt	Year	Flour s/cwt	Sugar s/cwt
1700	20.4	60.7	1723	8.8	36.9	1746	9.1	47.2	1769	15.0	52.7
1701	21.5	68.5	1724	11.0	29.4	1747	10.0	55.0	1770	15.7	51.8
1702	19.6	81.7	1725	12.1	33.4	1748	15.4	51.6	1771	17.5	50.9
1703	19.3	57.6	1726	12.5	36.4	1749	16.6	46.8	1772	20.3	49.2
1704	14.6	56.8	1727	11.5	32.6	1750	13.1	52.0	1773	18.9	50.0
1705	14.9	47.6	1728	10.0	35.2	1751	12.3	47.0	1774	18.1	55.6
1706	---	---	1729	10.7	35.0	1752	13.1	48.0	1775[4]	15.4	53.0
1707	---	33.0[2]	1730	11.6	32.1	1753	12.8	51.7	1784	24.8	62.3
1708	19.3	---	1731	8.0	33.2	1754	14.1	50.9	1785	22.4	52.0
1709	13.5	44.9	1732	8.2	33.4	1755	13.8	48.4	1786	21.3	55.9
1710	11.8	39.9	1733	8.8	28.9	1756	12.8	48.8	1787	19.1	53.8
1711	11.2	39.1	1734	10.5	29.2	1757	11.3	48.0	1788	16.1	54.8
1712	12.0	48.0[3]	1735	11.5	35.6	1758	12.3	47.7	1789	19.9	60.6
1713	16.1	60.3	1736	9.6	32.8	1759	14.6	45.2	1790	26.3	---
1714	16.8	58.6	1737	11.7	35.6	1760	15.0	47.9	1791	19.9	81.4
1715	10.3	40.8	1738	11.2	39.0	1761	14.8	49.1	1792	19.3	$14.46
1716	7.6	44.5	1739	8.0	38.1	1762	16.8	52.2	1793	23.6	$13.13
1717	8.4	44.2	1740	8.7	37.9	1763	16.9	49.8	1794	26.8	$10.50
1718	11.2	46.7[3]	1741	13.7	36.4	1764	12.8	48.7	1795	40.4	90.7
1719	11.4	37.0	1742	11.0	40.9	1765	13.5	52.9	1796	$6.40	$13.38
1720	9.3	35.5	1743	8.7	38.9	1766	14.8	55.7	1797	$4.54	$15.65
1721	8.8	33.1	1744	7.7	50.0	1767	17.2	49.4	1798	$4.17	$14.42
1722	8.9	31.9	1745	8.0	43.0	1768	16.9	46.4	1799	$4.92	$13.83

1. s/cwt = shillings local currency per 100 pounds. Note that in the 1790's values vary between s/cwt and $/cwt
2. Data for only one month available this year.
3. Data for only three months available this year.
4. No data available for 1776 - 1783.

TABLE 10
Average Annual Wholesale Prices
Charleston (SC)

Year	Flour £/cwt[1]	Sugar £/cwt	Year	Flour £/cwt	Sugar £/cwt	Year	Flour s/cwt	Sugar s/cwt	Year	Flour s/cwt	Sugar s/cwt
1745	---	14.50	1766	3.61	11.75	1780[2]	28.4	70.4	1790	42.2	52.1
1749[2]	---	4.08	1767	4.59	11.20	1781	40.4	65.6	1791	31.7	48.7
1750	---	5.87	1768	4.46	10.35	1782	39.3	70.3	1792	---	67.5[3]
1754[2]	---	12.00	1769	4.08	11.50	1783	---	30.3[3]	1793	---	54.0[3]
1755	---	10.80	1770	4.06	11.72	1784	36.5	25.2	1794	$5.35	52.3[3]
1761[2]	---	11.20	1771	3.95	10.00	1785	35.6	30.0	1795	s55.0[3]	60.0[3]
1762	4.26	11.20	1772	4.14	10.00	1786	39.9	42.1	1796	$7.17	63.5
1763	4.58	11.60	1773	4.87	---	1787	32.8	44.3	1797	$5.13	59.0
1764	3.75	9.46	1774	4.55	12.38	1788	28.8	40.5	1798	s23.9	64.0
1765	3.42	10.08	1775	4.58	11.88	1789	32.6	39.3	1799	s27.2	65.0

1. £/cwt = pounds local currency per 100 pounds. Note that units change to shillings/cwt in 1780 and $/cwt passim after 1794.
2. No data available for intervening years.
3. Data for only one month available.

TABLE 11
Average Annual Wholesale Prices
New York

Year	Flour s/cwt[1]	Sugar s/cwt	Year	Flour s/cwt	Sugar s/cwt	Year	Flour s/cwt	Sugar s/cwt	Year	Flour s/cwt	Sugar s/cwt
1748	21.6	44.5	1759	18.5	48.5	1770	16.9	65.0	1789	23.0	69.2
1749	17.4	41.3	1760	18.5	48.5	1771	19.6	53.0	1790	29.3	76.0
1750	13.8	50.2	1761	17.3	49.7	1772	22.2	53.0	1791	19.9	79.0
1751	14.3	47.9	1762	20.1	49.8	1773	21.6	52.5	1792	---	---
1752	14.7	47.9	1763	18.9	56.7	1774	19.5	63.3	1793	24.7	79.2
1753	14.7	50.4	1764	14.3	52.5	1775	17.6	64.0	1794	27.8	104.5
1754	15.9	49.2	1765	15.8	50.0	1776	16.8	101.5	1795	40.0	95.3
1755	16.0	49.7	1766	17.1	64.1	1785[2]	28.6[3]	50.8	1796	$7.08	---
1756	15.3	48.2	1767	19.8	56.0	1786	23.7	60.0	1797	$4.11	---
1757	14.1	47.7	1768	18.7	56.0	1787	22.8	59.0	1798	$3.71	---
1758	14.3	49.0	1769	17.0	57.8	1788	20.4[3]	70.0[3]	1799	$4.55	---

1. s/cwt = shillings local currency per 100 pounds. Note change to $/cwt in 1796 (flour).
2. Years 1777 - 1784, no data available.
3. Data for only one month available.

TABLE 12
Average Annual Wholesale Prices
Boston

Year	Flour s/cwt[1]	Sugar s/cwt	Year	Flour s/cwt	Sugar s/cwt	Year	Flour s/cwt	Sugar s/cwt	Year	Flour s/cwt	Sugar s/cwt
1752	15.7	---	1762	17.7	40.7	1772	20.0	40.6	1786	21.4	40.3[4]
1753	15.9	38.0[2]	1763	16.9	40.5	1773	19.3	38.8	1787	17.6	---
1754	16.3	44.2	1764	14.6	41.4	1774	18.6	43.2	1788	15.5	43.3[5]
1755	16.0	41.7	1765	14.3	40.9	1775	18.9	48.0[4]	1789	16.6	37.5
1756	15.9	39.6	1766	15.1	41.5	1776	22.4	59.8	1790	21.6[5]	47.5
1757	14.5	36.0	1767	17.3	43.0	1781[3]	30.3	50.3[2]	1791	16.2	54.0
1758	15.2	42.2	1768	16.9	39.2	1782	31.1	55.5	1792	15.4	---
1759	17.5	39.0	1769	15.3	42.9[2]	1783	26.6	51.6	1793	18.8	---
1760	17.1	40.7	1770	16.7	48.4[2]	1784	19.8	43.7	1794	20.6	75.0[5]
1761	16.6	40.8	1771	18.2	37.5	1785	19.7	42.7[5]	1795	34.4	64.3

1. s/cwt = shillings local currency per 100 pounds.
2. Data for only two months available this year.
3. No data for intervening years available.
4. Data for only one month available this year.
5. Data for only three months available this year.

Examples

**1. Inventory from Northampton County,
Pennsylvania, 1828; valued at $1,492.10 1/2.**

This type of inventory is an example of those easiest to handle. It falls within the range of Table 4 and it is valued in dollars. Converting the value to 1982 dollars is a simple matter of multiplying the stated value by the factor for 1828 (8.70):

$$
\begin{array}{r}
\$\ \ 1,492.10\ 1/2 \\
\times\ 8.70 \\
\hline
\$\ 12,981.31
\end{array}
$$

It is well worth noting that this inventory does not include any listings for buildings or land.

**2. Inventory from Albemarle County,
Virginia, 1790; valued at £ 60/8/5.**

This inventory is more difficult for two reasons: it predates Table 4, so no direct conversion is possible, and it is valued in £/s/d. It should be remembered that this is in current money of Virginia (not pounds sterling). Table 6 provides wages for Virginia for 1781, which is about as close as one can get; it is not likely that wages changed a great deal over this nine-year period. Note that in Table 6 all wages are given in terms of local currency; therefore, no differences in currency need to be addressed.

Converting £60/8/5 to pence:
$$(((60 \times 20) + 8) \times 12) + 5 = 14501$$
Wage rate is 2/0 per day which = 24 d/day
$$\frac{14501\ d}{24\ d/day} = 604.2\ days$$

This means it would have taken a common laborer 604.2 days, or about 2.32 years to earn this amount of money working 5 days per week. Again, this inventory makes no mention of any real property.

**3. Inventory from Northampton County,
Pennsylvania, 1793; valued at £4512/4/2.**

There are no wage rates for Pennsylvania given during this time period. Rather than go "out of state," let's use some commodity prices.

Table 9 gives the price of flour in Philadelphia during 1793 as 23.6 shillings per cwt. The current price of wheat flour is about $10.00 per cwt.

> Converting inv. value to pence:
> $$(((4512 \times 20) + 4) \times 12) + 2 = 1,082,930 \text{ d}$$
> Flour price (1793) in pence:
> $$23.6 \times 12 = 283.2$$
> How much flour could inv. value buy?
> $$\frac{1082930 \text{ d}}{283.2 \text{ d/cwt.}} = 3823.9 \text{ cwt.}$$
> Correction for relative food costs: [18]
> $$3823.9 \times 3 = 11,471.72 \text{ cwt.}$$
> How much would that flour cost today?
> $$11471.72 \text{ cwt.} \times \$10.00 \text{ per cwt.} = \$114,717.15$$

Once more, even though this estate has a large valuation, no real property is mentioned in the inventory.

4. Inventory from Boston, Massachusetts, 1693; valued at £933/18/4.

Wage rates for Boston are available for 1670 (Table 6), in which it is found that a common laborer made about 2/0 per day. Both inventory valuation and wage rates are in current money of Massachusetts.

> Valuation converted to pence:
> $$933 \times 20 + 18 \times 12 + 4 = 224,140 \text{ d}$$
> Labor rate of 2/0 = 24 d/day
> Amount of labor needed to earn 224140 d:
> $$\frac{224140 \text{ d}}{24 \text{ d/day}} = 9339.17 \text{ days}$$

This means that a common laborer in Boston would have had to have worked 9339.17 days or 35.9 years (5 days per week) to have earned this amount of money. Real estate in this inventory was valued at 297/6/-, or a little less than one-third of the total value.

---

[18] See p. 36.

5. Inventory from Northumberland County, Virginia, 1650; valued at 1231 lb. tobacco.

This inventory is an example of one of those valued in commodity money. Table 1 indicates that in 1649 tobacco was valued at 3 d sterling/lb. Hence the value of the estate in pence sterling was:

$$1231 \text{ lb. x } 3 \text{ d/lb.} = 3693 \text{ d}$$

The closest wage rate (geographically and temporally) is that for farm workers in Maryland (Table 7). They earned 2/6 sterling per day. Note that both values are in pence sterling.

$$\frac{3693 \text{ d}}{30 \text{ d/day}} = 123.1 \text{ days}$$

The value of this estate was therefore somewhat modest, requiring 123.1 days or about one-half year's labor to earn its equivalent.

6. Inventory from King and Queen Co., Virginia, 1700; valued at £91/8/2.

This man was a carpenter, and wage rates for carpenters in South Carolina are available for 1710 (Table 8). However, the inventory is valued in current money of Virginia and the wage rates are in current money of South Carolina. The rate is 4/0 per day (= 48 d/day). To convert this to its equivalent in Virginia money:

$$\frac{48 \text{ d/day}}{x \text{ d/day}} = \frac{161}{111} \text{ (Table 2, relating Virginia and South Carolina money to pound sterling)}$$

$$x = 48 \text{ x } (111/161) = 32.8 \text{ Virginia d/day}$$

Converting the value to pence and calculating as in example #4, we see that this inventory value was equivalent to about 2.6 years of work for a carpenter.

CHAPTER 3

WHAT DOES IT MEAN?

The time has come for that enlightened peek into the bathroom closet that was promised earlier. The data in Chapter 1 and the Glossary should have helped you figure out what the inventory listed, and Chapter 2 should have shed some light on the overall value of the estate, but it is usually possible to glean more than this.

How did people at the time (and your ancestor in particular) live? What were his skills and abilities, his interests? What kind of a person was he? These questions and many others both haunt and fascinate the family history researchers. They can sometimes be answered (although not usually directly) through a careful evaluation of his estate. While it must be admitted that some inventories (e. g. the ones consisting of three lines) say virtually nothing, it is usually possible to get some ideas. What, exactly, depends on the particular inventory and your own acumen in making deductions. Although this chapter may indeed give you some specific ideas on approaching this problem, it is more to be hoped that it will simply open your eyes to the possibilities. If you know to look for something, it is more likely that you will find it.

As has been the case earlier, the material in this chapter is presented by way of example. In each case the inventory given is an actual estate inventory—no "doctoring" has been done. In order to conserve space, some material not essential to the question at hand may have been omitted. When this occurs, a notation is made as to what has been left out. Line numbers (which did not appear in the original document) have been provided to facilitate references to specific entries in the inventory.

Example 1: Subsistence Living
Estate Inventory from Scituate, Plymouth County, Massachusetts [19]

A True Inventory of all the Real & personal Estate that Timothy White Late of Scituate Shoemaker Decd. dyed Seazed off which was Apprized by us the Subscribers this 10th day of March 1774.

waring apparel
two Guns, Desk, Looking Glass, Picturs Squar Table
one Tee Table, warming pan, Puter, Tin wair
7 old Chars, one Cradle, box Iiron & heters
5   bed bedsted & furniture in ye Lore [lower] Room, Trundlebed
bed bedsted & furniture in ye Chamber, Sute of Curtins & Rods
a Case draws, a Round Table, Six Chares
a Case of Bottles, a foot wheel and Great Do.
a Chest & a Small Do., Bread Trove, Hatt Case, 25 lb. of flax
10 4 Bushels of Rye, one Do. of wheet, 5 Do. of Barly
wool, three powder horns, 78 Skeens of woosted
35 Skeens of wooling Yarn, old Casks
25 lb. of Beef, two meel baggs, two lb. of Candles
25 Bushels of Corn, 20 lb. of Lather [leather], a Cod Line
15 Bible & books, 4 Pillebers [pillow beers],
3 Table Cloths, 9 Towels
120 lb. pork, puttatos, Iiron pot & Cittle
a pair Slice & Tongs, 2 Candle Sticks & Bellows
a Brass Cettle, Brass Skillet & Iiron Do., Tee Cettle
frying pan, Tost Iiron Gridiiron Chaffen Dish & Choping knife
20 Erthen wair, wooden wair, a meet Tubb
Shoemaking Tools, two-thirds of a Saddle & Bridle
pair andjirons, Spit, Handsaw, Draw Shave, brod ax
4 Augers, 6 Chisels Gouge Squar & bit
a narrow ax, one old hoe, one old Sythe
25 his Intrest in Spade dungfork & Ditch hook & betle & wedges
his Do. in Fork & Rakes, in Collar & Hames, in Chanes
his Do. in two plow Cops, in a Yoak, Cart and Cops
two Swine, his Intrest in Grinstone
his Intrest in a Yoak of oxen
30 three Cows, a two year old heffer, 3 Caves
his Intrest in a Horse, Ten Sheep
his Do. in Five Tun of hay
a Gundilo
Real estate £266/10/-

Total valuation: £375/1/2

[19] From a transcription appearing in Alice Hanson Jones, *American Colonial Wealth*, Vol. 2, 2nd ed. (New York: Arno Press, 1977), pp. 879-80. Line-by-line and intraline values have been omitted, as have been repetitions of "To" [to wit.].

The most obvious fact of this inventory is that it is a marvelous example of subsistence living. We read in the introductory statement that Timothy White was by profession a shoemaker. This fact is borne out by the listing of his tools (line 21) and raw materials (leather, line 14). He provided for his family in other ways as well. Note the fishing equipment mentioned: a cod line (line 14) and a gunalow (a heavy, flat-bottomed boat, often with a single sail; this was not a pleasure boat, but rather a work boat, line 33). He also did some farming.

Real estate valued at 266 pounds in this area at this time (data from other inventories) implies a house on about fifteen acres of workable land. In addition, farm produce (lines 9, 10, 14, 32) and animals (lines 28, 29, 30, 31) also support this assumption. Other self-sufficiency skills were also present. Many carpenter's tools are listed (lines 22, 23, 24), and the family probably provided much of its own clothing, evidenced by listing of materials (flax, line 9; wool, line 11; woolen yarn, line 12) and equipment (foot wheel and great wheel, line 8). The presence of ten sheep (line 31) and the large quantity of wool implies that they worked more in this material than in flax. The absence of tools for working flax (e.g. hackles, breaks) implies they probably did not raise flax or at least didn't work it themselves. Note also the absence of weaving equipment; wool can be knitted easily, while flax is generally too fine. Additional subsistence was probably provided by hunting (guns, line 2; powder horns, line 11).

It is worth noting separately that much of the more expensive and less frequently used farm equipment and animals (e.g. oxen) were owned jointly with at least one other party. This is shown by the listing of "his interest in" these (lines 25, 26, 27, 28, 29, 31). The hay for these animals was apparently also raised jointly, since he is credited with an interest in five tons of hay (line 32).

When one considers the matter, this is a very rational approach, especially if farming was not his prime means of earning a living. I should mention at this point that joint ownership of more expensive items is to be found in inventories from all parts of the country and during all time periods. Knowing this should help explain some otherwise odd kinds of entries one may encounter. For example, one of my ancestors was listed as having owned "half of a rifle gun." This did not mean that he owned only a part of a gun, but rather that he owned a half interest in one. I have also seen entries in inventories such as "half a cow" and "a third of a horse." If one knew no better, he might assume that these entries referred to a cache of meat rather than to live animals. Please note that the inventory cited here is somewhat unusual in actually specifying "an interest in;" the latter examples in this paragraph (without that phrase) are more typical.

More observant readers may have noted that another possession of this family is also described indirectly—their house. Note that in lines 5 and 6 mention is made of two rooms in the house (the lower room, line 5, and the chamber, line 6). From this it may be deduced that the house was most likely a two-story dwelling with one room on each floor. It is possible that there was a separate kitchen (that is simply not mentioned), but the reference to the chamber (which almost always refers to a second-floor bedroom), implying that there was only one bedroom on the second floor, argues against such an assumption. The layout of houses was fairly standardized at this time, and a house such as the one assumed here fits one standard pattern. Typical house layouts are discussed in more detail later.

Some genealogical suppositions can also be made on the basis of the data in this inventory. Timothy White was almost certainly married. The presence of large amounts of material and equipment for weaving implies that a woman lived here. It is not usual to find such amounts of this kind of material in a bachelor's household, unless he was a weaver by trade. There were probably children as well. Note the listing of a cradle (line 4). Considering the context, it is unlikely that this refers to a reaper's cradle for a scythe. Note also that there are beds in two rooms (lines 5 and 6) and that in one of these rooms there is also a trundle bed (line 5). Finally, one might also assume that Mr. White was literate, since not only a Bible but also other books are mentioned (line 15). Even illiterate people sometimes had a Bible, but they rarely had other books.

Example 2: House Layout and Real Estate
Estate Inventory from Marblehead, Essex County, Massachusetts [20]

This inventory is quite long and shows a man who was very successful in this world. The most important information different from that given in the previous example is the excellent description of the house and some genealogical information given. Most of the inventory has been omitted, with only those lines germane to the above-mentioned points being included.

Essex SS To the Hon. Benjamin Lynde Esqr. Judge of prob. &c. for said County we the Subscribers being appointed and Sworn as by warrant and Certificat thereon and hereunto Annexed doth appear to appraise the Estate of Doct. Humphrey Devereux, Late of Marblehead deceased, have done the same as followeth Vizt.

[20] Ibid., pp. 649-55.

Settingroom

one 8 day Clock, 7 glass picturs, Deverux arms, Hinch. Do.

Hall

Effegy of Doctr. Devreaux, do. mrs Devreaux, do. Boys

5   one fire glass, 5 musetants picturs, Henchmans Coat arms

Kitchen

old lumber in ye Celler

Hall Chamber

Settingroom Chamber

10   **Kitchen Chamber**

Garrett

Shop

Real Estate

The Mansion house wood house Chasehouse gardin &c.

15   a lott of Land adjoining ye mansion house with ye Barn

24   Acres Salt march in Chelsa adjoing Mrs. Henchmans Land.

All the listings in this inventory were divided according to the room in the house in which they were found. Each room name in bold given here actually incurred in the inventory. Putting these room names together, one can see that the house had two stories, with three rooms on each floor. This can be inferred from the fact that rooms on the second floor were invariably called "chambers" and each was usually further identified by naming the room on the first floor over which it lay. For example, the "kitchen chamber" was a bedroom on the second floor of the house directly above the kitchen. The first floor of the house contained a sitting room (equivalent to a parlor), a hall (the room in which the family would have spent most of their time), and a kitchen.

The most probable floor plan would be #10 in the examples given on the following page. As explained earlier, the second floor consisted of three bedrooms, one over each room on the first floor. The inventory also mentions a garrett, which would have been between the second story ceiling and the peak of the roof. In this particular house, it seems to have served the function of a modern attic, a collection point for infrequently used items. In some houses it might also have served as an additional bedroom. Food was also sometimes stored there, especially when the house had no pantry or buttery.

In this particular house, access to the cellar was probably through the kitchen, since cellar items are listed under the heading of "kitchen" (line 7). In other houses, access to the cellar was frequently through a cellar door outside the house. Although there is no way to be certain, the "shop" (line 12) may well have been a separate building. In more southern colonies this would almost have been the rule, but in New England it is varied. There were, however, several outbuildings. We see (lines 14 and 15) that there was a wood house, a chase house (for vehicles), and a barn.

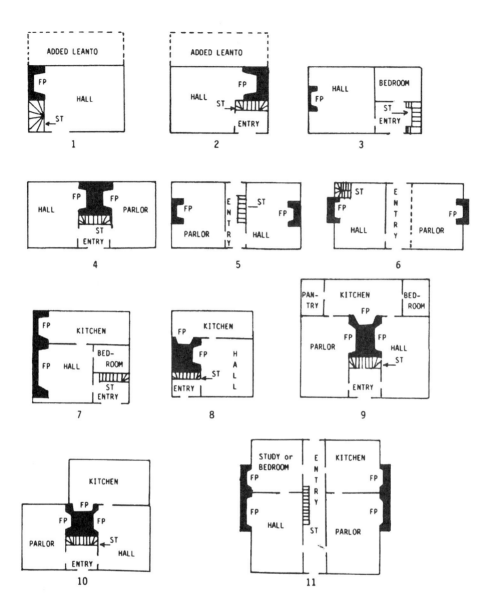

The above plans represent some of the standardized floor plans of houses during the Colonial Period; they constitute examples and not an exhaustive list. Walls and sections shown in dashed lines may or may not be present in specific houses. Each example is typical of a group or region as follows: 1) Rhode Island; 2) Connecticut; 3) Maryland; 4) New England; 5) Dutch; 6) Virginia; 7) Rhode Island; 8) Connecticut; 9) Massachusetts; 10) New England; 11) Maryland and Virginia (FP= fireplace. ST=stairs).

Some items mentioned are of genealogical significance. Note that the coats of arms of two families are mentioned (lines 2 and 5). Whether or not these families were actually entitled (by heraldic standards) to these is not the most important matter. While one should not be surprised at finding the arms of the Deveraux family, that of the Henchman family should lead one to believe that Mrs. Deveraux's maiden name may well have been Henchman. Note also that Dr. Deveraux owned land in Chelsea which adjoined that of a Mrs. Henchman. This could be a clue as to what town Mrs. Deveraux had come from. If the above suppositions are correct, one can also assume that her mother (but probably not her father) was still alive. As far as Dr. Deveraux's immediate family is concerned, we are led to believe that there were children and that they were most probably all boys; this is inferred from the "effegies" listed in line 4.

Although not included in the excerpts above, there was a supplementary listing of bonds and notes due the estate. Among the names were Humpy (Humphrey) Devereux and Ralph Devereux. They may be two of these sons, although there is no way to be sure based solely on the data given here. The importance of such listings is dealt with more fully in the next example.

Example 3: Family Structure and Relationships
Estate Inventory from Northampton County, Pennsylvania

The remarkable portion of this inventory is the listing of debts owned to and by the estate; only parts of these portions of the inventory are given below.

A true and Perfect Inventory and conscionable appraisement of all and Singular the Goods & Chattels, Rights & credits, Which Where [i.e. were] of Frederick Lerch the elder, late of Forks township County of Northampton, Yeoman, at [the] time of his death, to Wit. [Decr 22 1827]

Bonds, Notes and Book accounts . . .
    Anthony Lerch, due By a bond dated the 29th Janu 1812 Payable the
        15th April 1821
    William Lerch Balans on Bond Payable the 18th April 1825
    John Lerch Bond Payable the 1t Aprill 1827
5   Frederick Lerch by Note payable 1t Aprill 1826
    David Kammer Note Dated the 17t Octobr 1829
    Philip Lerch Note dated the 1t aprill 1829
    Jonas Lerch Note dated the 1t aprill 1829
    Henry Lerch Note dated the 19t Decembr 1823
10   George Kuhn Note dated the 5t June 1826
    Book accounts, as In Atwants [i.e. advance] of Legucys

Anthony Lerch In the land sold to him, horses Wagon Plows and Sundrees
John Lerch In the land sold to him, Hors, Blacksmith Tools and one Stove
William Lerch in the land sold to him, Horses Wagon Plow and Sandrees
Frederick Lerch In the land sold to him, one hore [sic] and one Stove
15 George Lerch In the land Sold to him, one hors Blacksmith Tools and
   Sandreas
Philip Lerch, two horses, Wagon, Plow and horse harnes one Stove
Jonas Lerch in land sold to him, one horse one stove
Henry Lerch, one hors, Wagon, Plow, Stove & San . . .
To his Taughter Elisabeth, Inter married to Peter Yeager, of house hold
20 Thomas Lerch two horses, Wagon and Body Plow harrow and harnes
Amounts paid to Widow as per Dower and to others
the Widow
Thomas Lerch
Susanna Lerch
25 Margratt Lerch
Christian Lerch

Frederick Lerch did not leave a will, and indeed the bulk of the papers dealing with the settlement of his estate deal with the inventory, a portion of which is given above. The potential value of these listings of names can be realized in this case, since data on his children was available from other sources. These children were (in order of birth): Anthony, John, William, Frederick, John George, Philip, Jonas, Elisabeth, Henry, Thomas, Susannah, Catharine, Andrew, Margaret, Christian, and Susannah [there were two children with this name; the first died before the second was born].

If one goes back and re-reads the material from the inventory, he finds that almost all of these children are mentioned at least once and sometimes twice. It is also worth noting that in the listings under "book accounts" those who are named are given almost exactly in birth order; the exception is that Elisabeth (line 19) follows Henry rather than preceding him. It is also of extreme importance to note that the name of Elisabeth's husband, Peter Yeager, is also given. Of equal significance is the fact that some children are not named, viz. Catharine, Andrew, and one of the Susannahs. It is known that all these children had died before 1827 (the date of the inventory).

Two other people are named as having been loaned money (David Kammer, line 6; George Kuhn, line 10). One might at first be led to assume that they were sons-in-law, although in this case it turns out not to have been a fact. Nevertheless, the appearance of such people (with different surnames) in such a situation certainly should be considered a clue, when other data is lacking. It may not always "pan out," but it can often lead one to check other materials that could prove such a relationship did exist. Along this line, I should point out that one of the major pieces of circumstantial evidence in proving that Elisabeth Schweitzer, wife of Frederick Lerch, was the daughter of Johannes Schweitzer is the fact that Frederick Lerch was listed as having been loaned money in the estate inventory of Johannes Schweitzer.

It was pointed out in the preceding paragraph and it is deserving of re-emphasis that finding someone's name in the estate inventory of another does not prove any biological relationship between them. To some extent the probability of their having been related depends on the cultural mores of the area or of the ethnic group involved. It turns out that for early Pennsylvania Germans it was much more probable that they would loan money to a relative than to others, and this was especially true when no formal, legal document concerning the debt (i.e. Note, Bond) was drawn up, as would be the case with "book accounts." When one encounters major exceptions to this practice it implies something about the loaner. It is assumed, for example, that Anthony Lerch (father of the Frederick Lerch above) was probably a very generous person. The inventory of this estate shows money loaned to a large number of people, many of whom are known not to have been relatives. One listing even shows that he had paid off a note owed by the minister of the church, which he had been unable to pay himself.

One final interesting fact can be inferred from the signatures of the administrators of the estate, given at the end of the inventory:

[tracing]

Note that these two men (sons of the deceased) signed their names in German script. This implies that they were educated in German rather than English. This fact might not mean much until one considers that they were of the second generation of this family to have been born in America; the family had arrived almost ninety years before. It would be reasonable to assume that German was still the household language among this family.

Example 4: Genealogical Data
Estate Inventory from York County, Pennsylvania [May 21, 1793]

Although this inventory does not add much that is different from that found in the previous example, it is interesting in terms of the amount of genealogical data it contains.

The following are accts which John Over decd has Charge his Children in a Small Book (which appd [i.e. appeared] to have made for the purpose) and are as follows

~ 54 ~

Maria, Intermaried to Mich¹ Swigert
2 Cows
Cash
BedCloath Pans and other Articles
5   Cash
Elizabeth Intermaried to Jnº Flickinger
1 Mare Sadle and Bridle which I allow her on acc¹ of her Staying with
    me over her age but Still to allow her one equal Shar with the Rest
    of my Children...
Cash
10 Cash for one Spinning Wheel
Potts Kittel & Lock
Catharine Intermaried to Peter Witter
15 2 Cows
Pewter Dishes & Basket
Cash for Spinning Wheel
one Iron Pot &
Pewter Ware
20 Iron Pott
BedCloath
Cash
Iron Pott

This inventory does not require any lengthy discussion; anyone can see the genealogical significance of finding the husband of each daughter listed. One should note, however, that the explanatory material in lines 7 and 8 gives some insight into the personal lives of these people that would probably have been otherwise lost. We can see that the daughter Elizabeth (who was probably the middle child, if the usual pattern is followed here) stayed with her father to care for him even after she had come of age. Her father was obviously grateful for this.

Example 5: Animals' Names and Names of Foreign Origin
Estate Inventory from Charles Town District, South Carolina [21]

A Just & True Inventory of the Esta. & Effects of Mr. William Freeman Decd. appraised by the under mentioned Subscribers this 18th day of Decembr. 1774.

1 Bay horse Steel 1 Gray Do.
1 Iron Grey Do. [horse] Bachelor

---

[21] *Ibid.*, 3:1511; only excerpts given, values omitted.

This extract from William Freeman's estate is noteworthy in that it points out the fairly common practice of listing animals by name. While knowing the names of the animals can be interesting in itself, it is more important that one realize that such a practice existed. In this example one might spend a great deal of time trying to figure out what a "horse steel" was. Although it has been mentioned earlier, it should be re-emphasized that one cannot count on the proper observance (by contemporary standards) of capitalization rules. In this case the proper noun "Steel" was indeed capitalized, but this is not always the case; note, for example, the improper capitalization of "bay," "iron," and "grey." An additional facet is added to this problem in inventories (in English) of non-English-speaking persons. The names of the animals are very commonly in the language of the deceased. The following entries occur in an inventory from Mississippi:

> a Cow charmante & her calf
> a Cow roughette

In these examples both of the cows are specified by name and, since the language commonly spoken in the area was French (many of the inventories are completely in French), the names of the cows are French.

Example 6: Genealogical Data on Slaves
Estate Inventory from Charles Town District, South Carolina [22]

Appraisement of the Effects of John Ainslie Esqr. at the Marons Plantation St. Paul Parish appraised by us at the request of John Hagard & John Parker Esqr. Executors April 21st 1774.

Negro man February Wife minah 4 Children
    Amilly Affy Osey & Bess—1300
Wench Cate—500
Man Abriam Wife Rinah & 4 Children
    Mary Lidia Billah & John—1500
Man adam wife Lucy 2 boys Adom & Peter—1100
5   wench Betty & Child [illeg.] Sarah—500
Man Adom wife nelly & Girl Hannah—700
wench Phillis 3 Chidn. Lucy Daphney & tirah—900
wench Ryrah 2 Chidn. Libby & Peg—800
man Jack & wife Florah—1000
10 Whench Sibbah—500 man simon—600
    man cyrus—30

[Note: numbers after dashes are values in pounds local currency.]

---

[22] Ibid., 3:1475; only excerpts given.

This excerpt demonstrates a common listing in inventories from southern states—slaves. While slaves (which were considered personal property and hence are listed among chattels) are usually listed by name, this example is less than typical in listing them by family groups. While knowing the number and types (i.e. men, women, children) of slaves may not seem particularly important at first glance, it does give one some idea of the relative wealth of the owner and the extent of his plantation. Listings of the type given above are, however, extremely important to any descendant of any of these slaves.

Since slaves had no legal status, very few vital records were generated regarding them. Without such family group listings, it is often extremely difficult to prove any relationships. Those who might be researching any of these slaves should also note that some of the material given in the opening statement to this inventory is also of great importance in knowing where to look for additional records: the name of the owner, the name of the plantation, and the location (St. Paul Parish). This data is critical in locating some of the other records commonly used in researching ancestors who were slaves (e.g. bills of sale).

Finally, the valuations of slaves can often give additional hints about the individual. As anyone who has read through many inventories soon discovers, slaves were quite valuable. Consequently, when one sees a valuation that is very low (e.g. Cyrus in line 10), he can be fairly certain that this person was probably old or had been incapacitated by disease or injury. Indeed, it is not uncommon for the inventorier to specify his reasons for placing a lower than usual value on a slave. This is especially true if it was due to incapacitation. When no reason is given, it is usually safe to infer age as the reason.

Example 7: Indentured Servants
Inventory of the estate of Joseph Frazer, a baker, from Philadelphia, Pennsylvania, dated April 19, 1774 [23]

> The time of a Dutch servant man, named Jacob Saunders 3..8 & 20 days
>   [i.e. 3 years, 8 months, 20 days]
> do. a Dutch servant woman, named Katharine Sobst 4..6.. & 2 days
> do. of Wm. McGwen, a boy for 5..11.. & 22 days
> do. of Patrick Connally, a servant man 4 mo. & 20 do.

This example is similar to the previous one in that servitude is involved in the excerpt presented. The difference is, of course, one of voluntary vs. involuntary servitude. This distinction is a legal one, and one

---

[23] Ibid., 1:271; only excerpts given, values omitted.

should not assume that every indentured servant entered into servitude voluntarily. It was often a matter of necessity, or in the case of children, of having it thrust upon them. Many of those who did indeed begin voluntarily, later became involuntary because of mistreatment.

There were basically three ways by which one might become a bound servant. Prior to departure for America one might enter into an agreement with the ship's captain, an agent of a person in America, a fellow emigrant, etc., in which he agreed to work for so many years in return for the payment of his passage. One might go to America and upon arrival, allow himself to be sold for so many years' servitude in return for the buyer's paying his passage. People in this last category were more properly referred to as "redemptioners."

The third way involved apprenticeships. A child might apprentice himself to a craftsman for a fixed number of years in order to learn a craft; in return the craftsman got cheap help. The "children" who apprenticed themselves were usually in reality teenagers or young adults. The child (and this was more often the case for young children) might also "be apprenticed" to a craftsman by his parents. Although the parents often received a payment, it should not be inferred that they were selling their children for profit. Frequently parents of modest economic means could not support all their children properly, and many of them saw this as a way in which the child's lot in life would be improved by his learning a marketable trade. Orphans or illegitimate children might be apprenticed by the state. Those interested in more detailed information on bound servitude, both of indentured servants and of slaves, should refer to Warren M. Billings, *The Old Dominion in the Seventeenth Century: A Documentary History of Virginia 1606-1689* (Chapel Hill, N.C.: University of North Carolina Press, 1975), pp. 127-174.

Regardless of the way in which the indenture came about, the result was a legal contract calling for a fixed number of years of bound servitude. Such contracts were considered legal debts owed to the estate of a deceased person, just as bonds and notes were. Since the contract was for a fixed period of time, only the amount of time still to be served was considered when placing a value on it for the inventory. This can be seen in the example above where the servants had times remaining from over five years to less than five months. These contracts could be inherited by the heirs or assigns of the deceased or could be sold to third parties. It should be noted that not all black or mulatto servants were necessarily slaves; those who were free had as much right as whites to indenture themselves. Although non-white indentured servants are often identified by race, it is a simple matter to distinguish them from slaves: if a time period is specified, they were indentured.

Some mention needs to be made of those inventories which include the names of people who bought items when an estate was auctioned off. In some instances such sales were recorded in a separate document, but frequently they are simply incorporated into the inventory itself. When such records are available they can add much to one's knowledge of the deceased. The most obvious thing gained is a listing of the neighbors. Especially during the earlier time periods when traveling was not easy, the people who attended these auctions were those who lived nearby. Such information can sometimes help identify the location of the deceased's property more exactly than some other documents. Even deeds often specify no more than the county and township. The exact boundaries are frequently given in terms of rocks or trees, none of which does the modern researcher any good since they have long since disappeared. One should also keep in mind that relatives were probably also among those attending the auction. It is especially worthwhile to note anyone with the same surname as the deceased.

Those inventories that include both an appraised value and the amount actually obtained at auction can give some insights into the economic situation in the area at the time. For example, if most of the items were sold for amounts far below the appraised values, it implies that money was tight. The sale of certain items far above the appraised value probably indicates that they were in short supply in the area. Similar ideas of the relative availability of certain items can be gleaned from any inventory (even without the auction data) by noting whether they were valued above the norm. To make such decisions, one must of course be familiar with the average values of different items at different times, but for the period around the time of the Revolutionary War the task has been made much easier by the publication of Alice Hanson Jones' *American Colonial Wealth* (see bibliography). Volume 3 of this work contains statistical breakdowns of the values of different items found in inventories throughout the original thirteen colonies.

How can one best approach an inventory to get the most from it? The most fundamental thing is to read the inventory critically; that is, think about each item that is mentioned and ask yourself what its presence implies. The answer may well be "nothing," but more often than not, it will tell you something. Consider items that form natural groups; for example, materials and tools associated with a particular endeavor, such as weaving. Thinking of such items as groups can help you notice something that is often as important as what is mentioned—what is **not** mentioned. If some basic piece of equipment is not listed, consider the implications of its absence. Make particular note of any people's names mentioned; these are very often important. Try to envision how the inventory was made. Does it seem that the inventoriers proceeded from one room to the next? What does this tell you about the layout of the house and outbuildings? Be on the lookout for any parenthetical comments made by the inventoriers. These may be as obvious as an explanatory note, or as subtle as the use of an odd and otherwise redundant adjective. Are there listings of large amounts of unusual (relative to the general nature of the items in the inventory) materials? These may indicate a sideline occupation. Make note of large numbers of even common items; a large number of beds in a house implies a large number of people to use them. In general, think about everything. Take nothing for granted.

CHAPTER 4

THAT'S A WORD?

It often happens that one reads a word in an inventory correctly without realizing it. This is usually due to the fact that the word is unfamiliar, either because it is no longer used or because it is a part of the jargon of some occupational group. It is the purpose of the glossary in this chapter to provide one with a listing of some of the more commonly encountered words that fall into these categories. It must be emphasized that this list should not be considered exhaustive. It has been compiled primarily by reading a large number of inventories and extracting words that the author felt worthy of inclusion.

Since the list does not include all possible words, it would be worthwhile to explain briefly how one goes about figuring out an unfamiliar word. This will provide the reader with a method by which he can approach unfamiliar words that are not found in this list. The first thing one must realize is that in standard reference works (dictionaries, etc.) the word will be listed under its currently accepted spelling. This means that one may have to try a variety of spellings phonetically similar to that given in the inventory. One cannot assume that the spelling given in the inventory is the correct one. It also helps to use a little imagination in doing this. Remember that parts of words are often left out (especially final consonants); single words are sometimes broken apart; and phrases are sometimes combined into a single word. Various aspects of phonetics have been discussed in detail in Chapter 1.

Secondly, the reference material used must be detailed enough to include uncommon words. This means that the standard desktop or even collegiate dictionary is rarely sufficient. One must use an unabridged dictionary. The best dictionary to use is *The Oxford English Dictionary*, a multi-volume set available in the reference department of most libraries. The advantage of this and other unabridged dictionaries is that they include specialized words (occupational jargon), archaic and obsolete words, and many dialectic forms. It should be noted, however, that they do not always include local slang terms (yes, they existed in the past). For these one must often turn to books dealing with specific genres such as kitchen utensils, Quaker furniture, old farm equipment, etc. In areas such as eastern Pennsylvania and southern Louisiana where most people spoke a non-English language, foreign language dictionaries may have to be consulted to rule out the possibility that the word is non-English.

In the listings that follow, some abbreviations and symbols have been used. They are:

1) A slash (/) separates two forms of the same word, both of which are considered acceptable spellings; e.g. froe/frow.
2) Letters enclosed in parentheses may be included or omitted in any particular use of the word given; e.g. batt(e)ry could appear as battery or battry.
3) An equals sign (=) indicates that the word has the same meaning as the word that follows; check the entry for that second word.
4) "Var." means that the word listed is a variant of the word that follows; again, see the entry for the second word.
5) "Pron." means "pronounced." Pronunciation is defined only for those words pronounced significantly differently from the way they are spelled. The phonetic spellings for such words are cross-indexed. A list of symbols and abbreviations is found at the end of the listings.

Glossary of Uncommon Words

Aberdeen
a breed of beef cattle.

Adz(e)
an edged tool with the blade at a right angle to the handle; used for achieving a flat or hollowed surface on wood. Of various types: carpenter's, American = shipwright's, cooper's, gutter (lipped or rounded blade), foot.

Alamode
a thin, glossy silk fabric.

Alamode pot
a pot for stewing pot roast.

Albatross
a light woolen fabric.

Alchemy
a golden-colored alloy, usually containing brass.

Alembic
a vessel or furnace used in distillation.

Allepine
a type of cloth, perhaps refers to the Allepo district of Syria.

Alt-azimuth
a navigational instrument for deducing altitudes and azimuths.

Alum
a chemical ($KA1(SO_4)_2 . 12 H_2O$) used to clarify water, in baking powders, and medicinally (internally as an emetic and topically as an astringent).

Anderson's (Scotch) Pills
a patent medicine (q.v.).

Andiron
a metal device for use in fireplaces to support logs and thereby allow for better air circulation.

Anemometer
a gauge for measuring the speed and direction of the wind.

Aneroid barograph/barometer
an instrument for measuring and recording variations in atmospheric pressure.

Angus
a breed of beef cattle.

Anise seed water
probably anisette, a liqueur flavored with anise.

Aniseed
var. of anise seed.

Anker
a liquid measure; in the U.S. about ten gallons. Avoid confusion with "anchor."

Apothecary chest
a piece of furniture similar to a chest of drawers, but with many small drawers.

Appurtenances
apparatus, gear integral to something; refers to what is now called "accessories."

Aqua vitae
generic for any type of spiritous liquor.

Arab(ian)
a breed of horses known for speed, intelligence, and spirit.

Arballista
= cross-staff.

Argand lamp/burner
a lamp with a tubular wick that admits a current of air inside as well as outside the flame.

Argol
crude tartar.

Arkamy
var. of alchemy.

Armillary sphere
a navigational instrument.

Armoire
(pron. ar-mwahr´) a cupboard, wardrobe, or clothespress of large size and usually ornate.

Armor
although armor was used in America during its early days, by 1650 interest in it waned quickly; for a complete description of types, see Harold L. Peterson, in bibliography.

Arms
1) weapons; 2) coat of arms.

Arquebus
usually used to refer to any type of early firearm.

Arrack
a spirit distilled from rum and flavored with fruits or plants.

Arras (hanging)
any textile in tapestry weave; a rich fabric with inwoven figures or scenes.

Arrow-back chair
a chair or rocker in which the back spindles are arrow shaped.

Artificial horizon
an instrument for taking hydrographic sightings during conditions of poor visibility.

Ashes
hardwood ashes cleaned from fireplaces were often put in containers and saved until needed for making soap.

Astral (lamp)
an argand lamp (q.v.) so constructed that no interruption of the light upon the table is made by the reservoir containing the oil.

Astrolabe
a navigational instrument.

Auger
a tool for boring holes in wood; some types were intended to make holes in the ground.

Augsburg dial
a type of sundial used in navigation.

Awl
an instrument with a sharp point used for punching holes in cloth, leather, etc.

Ax(e)
an edged tool used for various wood cutting functions, depending on the type. Types: pole (? = post), post, broad, felling, split = holzaxt, trade, chisel, mortise, marking, barking, narrow (= felling), double-(= two-) bitted, boarding, mat (see mattock).

Axe pistol
a combination weapon: a flint or wheel lock pistol with an axe blade attached.

Axletree
a spindle or axle or a wheel.

Ayrshire
a breed of dairy cattle.

Azimuth compass
a form of compass divided into degrees, with vertical sights for taking the azimuth of a star.

Baby
a doll used by dressmakers to display samples.

Backbar
= chimney lug.

Back-staff
navigational instrument for determining the altitude of the sun.

Baculus
= cross-staff.

Badikins
= whippletrees.

Bagging hook
a large sickle.

Baiting sieve
a basket-like container for measuring out horse feed.

Baize
imitation felt made of woven, napped wool.

Bake-kettle
a Dutch oven.

Bale/bayle
a ship's bucket.

Baler
a machine for compressing and tying hay.

Balestilla
= cross-staff.

Banc-lit
a settle bed (q.v.).

Band
a neckband or collar worn like a cravat.

Bandbox
a box of pasteboard or thin wood, usually cylindrical.

Bandeau
a narrow band or fillet, usually for the hair.

Bandolier
a wide belt worn over one shoulder, used to carry ammunition.

Banian/banyan
a loose woolen shirt or jacket.

Banister-back chair
a chair in which the back is made up of vertical slats.

Bank
in household inventories, especially in German-speaking areas, a bench; cf. banc-lit.

Bannock
an oblong wooden board, sometimes with a perpendicular handle attached to the back; when propped up beside a fire, used for baking cornmeal cakes.

Banyan
1) a cotton textile; 2) a type of men's dressing gown; 3) = banian.

Barb
a breed of horses related to Arabian, known for speed and endurance.

Barbados spirits/liquor
rum.

Barge
a flat-bottomed freight boat for inland waterways or for loading and unloading ships.

Bark
1) a sailing vessel with three or more masts, square rigged except the aftermast, which is fore-and-aft rigged; 2) a tanner's tub.

Bark cloth
a crinkled woolen fabric.

Bark mill
a machine for grinding bark (usually oak) for use in tanning hides.

Bark spud
a tool for removing bark from logs to hasten drying.

Barkentine
a sailing vessel with three or more masts, the foremast square rigged, the others fore-and-aft rigged.

Barking iron
a tool for removing bark to be used in tanning.

Barley hummeller
a tool for pounding barley.

Barleycorn
a checked fabric.

Barlow knife
a type of jackknife.

Barometer
an instrument for determining atmospheric pressure.

Barouch
a vehicle similar to a landau (q.v.) but with only half a folding top.

Barque
= bark, definition #1.

Barragon
probably a type of cloth.

Barré
a fabric with stripes of different colors.

Barrel
as a unit of liquid or weight measure, it varied according to the contents; e.g. 1 barrel of flour = 196 pounds.

Barrel-back
a corner cupboard or a settle (q.v.) whose back is curved, thus resembling the staves of a barrel.

Barrow
1) = handbarrow; 2) a castrated male hog.

Bartmann bottle
= bellarmine.

Basinet
a small wooden bowl.

Basket-spit
a spit with a basket of iron straps in the center, into which the meat is put.

Bateman's (Pectoral) Drops
a patent medicine (q.v.).

Bath metal
any of several varieties of brass.

Batiste
a very light cotton or woolen fabric of high quality.

Bat(t)eau
a double-ended boat with a V-bottomed hull, forty to fifty feet long; used on inland waterways.

Batt(e)ry
any metal article made by hammering.

Battle lantern
a lantern used to light ships' decks.

Battledore
1) a beetle (q.v.) or bat used in washing and smoothing clothes; 2) a raquet used with a shuttlecock in a badminton-like game; 3) a hornbook (q.v.).

Bay
1) a color, brown or red-yellow in hue, of low saturation and brilliance; 2) an animal, especially a horse, of bay color; 3) (usually plural) baize (q.v.) or a worsted fabric similar to baize but finer.

Bayadere
a barré fabric of brilliant colors, originally from India.

Bayberry
a tree whose fruit contains a wax used in candle making.

Bayle
= bale.

Beaker
a cup or glass for drinking.

Beakiron
1) the horn of an anvil; 2) a small anvil having a horn; a bickern.

Beam
literally the bar of a balance, from the ends of which the scales are suspended; sometimes used for the whole balance.

Bearing compass
a compass for taking bearings from seamarks.

Beaver cloth
a woolen cloth with a long nap.

Bec d'ane
a two-headed tool used for cutting rough mortises and tenons.

Becker
a wooden dish.

Becket
a rope handle.

Bed
usually used to refer to what is now called a featherbed. This is especially true if used with the term "bedstead," which is the piece of furniture now called a bed.

Bed warmer
a covered metal pan with a long handle into which hot coals could be placed to pre-warm sheets before going to bed.

Bedpan
1) a device similar to today's bedpan; 2) a bed warmer.

Bedroom
properly refers to a sleeping room on the first floor of a house; cf. chamber.

Beetle
a large wooden hammer.

Bell glass
a glass dome used to protect seedlings.

Bell metal
a variety of bronze consisting of three to four parts copper to one part of tin.

Bellarmine
a stoneware jug with a bearded face or mask embossed on it.

Bellows
a device for blowing air on a fire.

Bellus
= bellows.

Belongings
sometimes used in the sense of appurtenances (q.v.).

Belt loom
a type of small loom for weaving a band of material.

Bench table
= hutch table.

Bengal
a striped muslin fabric.

Bengaline
a corded fabric made of silk and wool.

Benjamin
1) a close-fitting men's coat; 2) a corrupted form of benzoin (q.v.).

Benjoin
variant of benzoin.

Benton's True & Genuine British Oil
a patent medicine (q.v.).

Benzoin
a balsamic resin from the tree *Styrax benzoin*, used medicinally as a stimulant and expectorant and in perfume and incense.

Betty lamp
a small shallow recepticle to hold tallow, grease, or oil, into which a wick extends; it is usually suspended from a hook and chain.

Bevel (guage)
a carpenter's tool used for copying and making angles (bevels).

Bible box
a type of writing box.

Bicker
a small, shallow wooden tub.

Bickern
= beakiron 2).

Biggin
1) a child's cap; 2) a hood or nightcap; 3) an early type of coffee percolator.

Billhook
1) any of various styles of cutting tools with a hook-shaped point; 2) a short-handled swinging knife.

Binnacle clock
a shipboard clock to show nautical watches.

Bird spit
a footed pan to catch drippings with a hood for roasting small birds.

Bird's eye
any of various types of cloth with a bird's eye pattern.

Bit
1) a piece of harness that fits into a horse's mouth; 2) a boring tool used with a brace.

Bitter Stomach Worm Drops
a patent medicine (q.v.).

Bitters
a liquor in which a bitter herb, leaf, or root has been macerated; used as a mild tonic or stimulant to increase the appetite or improve digestion.

Bittlin
a milk bowl of wood, pewter, glass, or pottery.

Black jack
= jack, definition #2.

Blanket box
a chest with no drawers.

Blind briole
probably a piece of harness that has blinders attached; the blinders are pieces of leather that block the horse's peripheral vision.

Block
a grooved pulley encased in a frame or shell which is provided with a hook, eye, etc., by which it may be attached to an object; a rope runs through the pulley; used to change the direction of an applied force and provide mechanical advantage.

Block Island boat
a fishing vessel tapering at both ends, having two masts, both fore-and-aft rigged.

Bloomery
a furnace or forge in which wrought-iron is made.

Blubber pot
a large, cast-iron cauldron for rendering blubber.

Blue
1) any blue pigment or dye; 2) bluing (usually powdered indigo) for use in the laundry to "whiten" cottons.

Blunderbuss
a short gun or large calibre with a wide, flaring muzzle.

Boar
a male hog.

Board cloth/clothes
a table cloth.

Boarding axe
a weapon used during boardings in naval battles.

Boatswain's whistle/pipe
a whistle used on ships to signal various events.

Bobbin
1) a piece of bone, ivory, or wood on which thread is wrapped; used in making bobbin lace and in weaving; 2) a fine cord or narrow braid.

Bodice
1) an inner garment stiffened with whalebone; a corset; 2) a tight-fitting garment reaching from bust to waist.

Bodkin
1) a dagger; 2) a sharp, pointed tool used like an awl or a coarse needle.

Bohea
(pron. bow´ hay) a superior grade of Chinese black tea.

Bolster
a cushion or pad.

Bolting cloth
a very finely woven silk fabric.

Bombard
a large leather drinking vessel; same as "jack" 2) but larger.

Bombasine
= bombazine.

Bombazine
a twilled fabric of silk or cotton warp and worsted filling; when dyed black, often used for mourning.

Bontine/bonting
a thin cloth of cotton or wool, often used for flags.

Boot jack
a V-shaped device for removing boots.

Bootlegger's pistol
a percussion cap, box-lock pistol.

Bore-staff
a loom attachment used to tighten the warp.

Boston rocker
a type of rocking chair.

Bosun/bowson
phonetic spelling of boatswain (q.v.).

Boucanier
= buccaneer.

Bourette
1) a silk, cotton, or linen yarn with nubs or knots in it to give it a rough appearance; 2) cloth made from such yarn.

Bow front
used alone, usually refers to a piece of furniture, such as a chest of drawers, with a convex front.

Box iron
a smoothing iron with an inner chamber to hold hot coals.

Brace
1) a crank-shaped handle used with various bits (q.v.) for boring holes in wood; 2) a pair or couple.

Brace(d)-back chair
a type of Windsor chair with two extra bracing spindles for the back.

Braid loom
a type of small loom for weaving straps, etc.

Braising pan
= brazier.

Brake/break
1) a large, heavy harrow (q.v.); 2) an instrument for breaking flax stems.

Branch
1) a part of a chandelier; seems also to have been used for candelabra.

Brandreth/brandlethe/brandlet
a tripod to support a pot or kettle above embers; a framework, generally of iron.

Brass
1) an alloy of tin and copper; 2) colloquial for a brass, copper, or bronze coin.

Bras(s)er
= brazier.

Brawls
a blue and white cotton cloth from India.

Brazero
= brazier.

Brazier
1) an open pan on a footed base for braising or broiling; 2) any small portable stove.

Brazilette
a type of redwood (q.v.).

Breast
= mouldboard.

Breast plate
1) a piece of armor; 2) a strap that runs across a horse's breast.

Breeches
a pair of trousers, usually coming just below the knee.

Brewster chair
a 17th-century chair with turned spindles in the back and below the front of the seat.

Brick
Types: statue = small = common, place, stock, Dutch = Flemish, English, copying.

Brig
a seagoing vessel with two masts, square rigged.

Brigandine
an armored vest.

Brigantine
a seagoing vessel with two masts, one square rigged and the other fore-and-aft rigged.

Brilliantine
a very closely woven cloth of cotton and angora wool.

Brimstone
sulphur.

Brindle
a brindled (q.v.) animal.

Brindled
having dark streaks or spots on a gray or tawney background.

Bristol blue
a dark blue, translucent glass.

Bristol glass
an opaque white glass.

British Oil
a patent medicine (q.v.).

Broadaxe
an axe with a large, flat blade with a chisel edge on one side only; used for squaring logs into beams.

Broadcloth
a fine napped woolen cloth, usually of double width.

Brocades
silk fabric with a raised pattern of figures in colors.

Broom
phonetic variant of brougham.

Brougham
(pron. brow´um, browm, or broom) a light closed carriage with seats inside for two or four and a driver outside; the front wheels are smaller than the rear wheels.

Brown Bess
a nickname for the standard British musket during the French and Indian and Revolutionary Wars.

Brown Swiss
a breed of dairy cattle.

Brussels
used alone, usually refers to Brussels lace.

Brussels carpet
a looped pile carpet made of various colored worsted yarns in a linen web foundation.

Brussels lace
a kind of bobbin lace in which the pattern is made first, the threads following the curves of the pattern, and the ground is put around it afterwards.

Buccaneer musket
a musket, 5 1/2 feet long; sometimes used on ships. A "**demi-buccaneer**" is a smaller version.

Buck
1) lye; hence a **bucking tub or buck tub** is a lye tub, a tub in which clothes, thread, or yarn are washed in a lye solution for its bleaching action; 2) the body of a wagon, especially the front part; 3) a hay sweep; 4) a male Negro or Indian.

Buck rake
a tractor-mounted hay sweep.

Buckboard
a type of wagon with a flat bed and one seat near the front.

Bucket bench
a piece of furniture with a cupboard, usually closed, below, and a raised shelf with a gallery around it.

Buckle
types: shoe, spur, belt, baldric, stock, knee, hat.

Buckling comb
a comb for a kind of crisp curl (called a buckle).

Buckram
1) a fabric of fine linen or cotton for clothes; 2) a coarse cloth of linen or hemp, stiffened with sizing or glue; used in hats or garments to keep them in shape; also used in bookbinding.

Buff coat
a type of leather armor.

Buffin
a coarse woolen fabric.

Bull stag
a castrated bull.

Bullet mold
a metal mold into which molten lead is poured to make bullets.

Bullseye lamp
a wicked lamp with 1 or more glass lenses around the flame to concentrate the light.

Bumper
a large drinking vessel.

Bun
= rump.

Bungstart
a mallet with a long flexible handle; used for putting bungs in the bungholes of barrels.

Bunt
a device for sifting meal.

Bunting
a thin, coarse woolen fabric.

Buret
a drinking vessel.

Burgundy
a type of red wine.

Burlap
a coarse fabric of jute or hemp.

Burnt
applied to pottery, fired.

Burnt umber
see umber.

Burying
see mourning.

Bushel
a unit of measure, the exact amount of which (in weight) varies with the material.

Busk
a stiffening material used in corsets.

Bussa pot
a pot for preserving pilchards (a type of fish).

Butt
1) a large cask; 2) a unit of measure equivalent to two hogsheads, but the size varied with time and place.

Butter bat
a wooden paddle for working butter.

Butterfly table
a drop-leaf table whose swing-out leaf supports resemble butterfly wings.

Butteris/buttress
a farrier's tool; used to trim hooves.

Buttery
originally a place where beer, ale, butter, etc., were kept; later it came to mean the same as pantry.

Button
some buttons, especially fancy ones, were not sewn to clothes but rather kept free so they could be used with different clothes; cf. those buttons used today with formal wear.

Cabbage plane
now usually called a "kraut cutter": a device for shredding cabbage.

Cable net
a coarse-meshed cotton net used for curtains.

Caboose
an open-air cooking oven.

Cabriolet
originally a light, one-horse carriage with two wheels and a single seat; later a one-horse carriage with two seats and often a canopy or extension top.

Caddis/caddice
1) floss silk, cotton wool or lint, especially a padding; 2) worsted yarn; crewel; a kind of worsted ribbon or binding; 3) a heavy woolen twill.

Caddow
a coarse woolen quilt or coverlet.

Cairn
a pile or stones, often used as a boundary marker.

Calabash
a water dipper, bottle, basket, or other small utensil, usually made from the dried shell of a calabash or other gourd.

Calash
1) a light carriage with low wheels and a top or hood that could be raised or lowered, four seats inside, and a separate driver's seat; 2) a hood for a carriage that could be opened or closed; 3) a woman's hood, made on hoops and thrown back.

Caldron
= cauldron.

Calico
originally any of a large number of cotton fabrics, found plain or in patterns other than the commonly known small-figured multicolored prints.

Calimanco
a glossy woolen cloth, ribbed or plain.

Caliver
an early firearm, light enough to be fired without a rest.

Calking
applied to various tools, such as mallets, irons, hooks; used for adding or removing calking between ships' timbers.

Calomel
a laxative, usually mercurous chloride.

Camblet
any fabric resembling one made of camel's hair.

Cambric
a well-bleached, fine linen or cotton fabric.

Cambridge roller
a roller made up of a large number of rings.

Camlet
= camblet.

Can
1) a large vessel from which cups are filled; 2) a cup made of metal.

Can hook
a device consisting of a short rope or jointed bar with flat hooks at each end for lifting barrels or casks by the ends of the staves.

Canal boat
a wide, shallow-draft boat used in canals; propelled by poling or pulled by mules from the bank.

Canal horn
a horn, usually of brass, used on narrowboats.

Canary
a sweet wine, similar to madeira.

Candle-arm
= sconce, definition #1.

Candle beam
a rude type of chandelier consisting of

a metal or wooden hoop with candle holders.

Candle box
a container for storing candles; they ranged in size from the large capacity boxes used for a long-term storage to the smaller size, holding a few candles for ready access as replacements.

Candle-mo(u)ld
a group of metal cylinders into which melted tallow or wax is poured around a wick to make candles.

Candle-prong
= sconce, definition #1.

Candlestand
a piece of furniture to hold candles; similar to what was later called a lampstand. The post was often made adjustable by being a screw, ratchet, etc.

Cannister
an instrument used by coopers in racking off wines.

Cannonball bed
a bedstead with heavy posts, the finials of which are shaped like a cannon ball.

Canoe
a boat similar to today's canoe but often much bigger.

Cant hook
a wooden pole with a metal hook attached by a hinge about one-third of the way from the end; used for rolling logs.

Canvas
a heavy linen or cotton fabric.

Capillaire
1) a syrup prepared from maidenhair fern; 2) any syrup flavored with orange flowers.

Capuchin
a type of cloak.

Caraco
a type of jacket for women.

Carbine
a firearm similar in size to a musketoon (q.v.), sometimes rifled.

Carboy
a large glass bottle encased in a box or wickerwork.

Card
1) a piece of leather, sometimes mounted on wood, with many fine wire teeth; used to disentangle fibers of wool, flax, or cotton prior to spinning; 2) a map.

Card table
a small table with a single leaf supported by swing-out legs.

Cardinal
a woman's hooded cloak.

Cardus
probably a type of decorative cording or ribbon.

Carmine
a crimson or scarlet pigment and dye made from cochineal.

Carnelian
a mineral of various shades of red; it polishes well and is hard and tough.

Caroteel
var. of carrtrell.

Carpenter's square
a type of square (q.v.).

Carriage wrench
a wrench for removing or tightening the hub nuts of a carriage.

Car(r)t(r)ell
a unit of measure varying with the material involved.

Cartouch(e)
1) a cartridge of paper; 2) a cartridge box.

Cartridge box
a pouch, usually of leather, in which bullets, wads, and other accoutrements for a gun are carried.

Cartridge paper
1) a thick stout paper for making cartridge cases; 2) a rough tinted paper for covering walls; 3) an inferior grade of drawing paper.

Carver chair
a chair similar to a Brewster chair (q.v.) but without the turned spindles below the front of the seat.

Case
the term is more often used of what is now called a display case or presentation case. It does not usually mean a large number; e.g. a case of pistols usually meant two in a presentation case.

Case knife
literally any knife kept in a sheath or case, but often refers to a carving knife.

Casement fabric
any light fabric suitable for curtains.

Cassock
1) a long, loose coat or gown worn by men and women; 2) any of several styles of ecclesiastical garb.

Caster
1) a slang term for cloak; 2) (also pron. castor) a vial, cruet, or other small vessel to hold condiments at the table; 3) a stand to hold a set of cruets; 4) a type of hat, originally of beaver.

Castover
probably related to "caster," meaning cloak.

Cat
a double tripod having six legs, on three of which it rests however it is placed; used for holding plates, pots, etc., over a fire.

Catrich
var. of cartridge.

Cattail
a plant found in marshy areas, the roots of which are edible, the dried leaves used for weaving baskets, and the shredded tops for stuffing ticks, etc.

Caudle
a warm drink for sick persons, especially a mixture of wine or ale with eggs, bread, or gruel, sugar, and spices.

Caul
1) a covering net for the head; 2) the netting of a wig; 3) the netting at the back of a woman's cap.

Cauldron
A large kettle, often with tripod legs on the bottom.

Cellar
1) a case, especially for holding bottles; 2) a receptacle; as a box, placed beneath something to contain a supply of some necessary article (oil, tools, etc.).

Cellaret
a case or sideboard for a few bottles of wine or liquor.

Chaff bed/bag
a bed (q.v.) filled with chaff as insulating material.

Chaff horse
apparatus to hold hay to be cut up for animal feed; functioned like today's paper cutter.

Chaffern
= chafing dish.

Chafing dish
1) a vessel for heating water; 2) a vessel to keep anything hot: a dish over a portable grate containing coals.

Chain
1) a measuring line of 100 links used in surveying; 2) a unit of measure, the length of a surveying chain, sixty-six feet.

Chair
types: feather-back, slat-back, rib-back, banister-back, fiddle-back, brace(d)-back, comb-back, ladder-back, arrow-back, easy, parlor, dining (room), fancy, drawing room, Brewster, carver, corner, night (q.v.), slipper (q.v.), elbow (q.v.), Windsor (q.v.).

Chair wheel
a type of spinning wheel whose frame resembles a chair; it has a divided treadle so that both feet can be used to operate it.

Chaise
1) a two-wheeled carriage for one or two persons with a calash top and the body suspended on leather straps; 2) a similar four-wheeled pleasure carriage; 3) loosely, any light or pleasure carriage.

Chaldron
1) a unit of measure for coal, about thirty-two bushels; 2) a unit of weight = about 2,500 lbs.

Chalk-line
a length of cord impregnated with chalk, which leaves a straight line mark when fastened down at both ends and snapped against something.

Challie/challis/chally
a light woolen fabric.

Chamber
a sleeping room on the second floor of a

Chamber (continued)
house; probably also used for the whole second floor. Often specified by the room over which it lay; e.g. hall chamber, kitchen chamber.

Chamber pot
a bedchamber vessel for urine.

Chamblet
= camblet.

Chambray
a plain fabric with one color in the warp and another in the weft.

Chamfer knife
a tool shaped like a froe, but designed to be pulled rather than driven.

Chandler
a candlemaker.

Charger
a large flat dish or platter for carrying meat.

Chariot
a closed, four-wheeled, fixed-top vehicle, basically the back half of a coach, with a driver's seat outside in the front.

Chased
(usually used of metals) ornamented by embossing, cutting away of parts, or setting with gemstones.

Chatelaine
an ornamental hook, pin, or clasp worn at a woman's waist, having chains attached for keys, trinkets, a watch, or a purse.

Chattel
personal (usually moveable) property, as opposed to real property (q.v.).

Chebacco
a partially decked fishing boat, hull tapering at both ends, and having two masts fore-and-aft rigged.

Chebobbin
a loosely fitted sled for hauling heavy loads, especially logs.

Cheese press
an apparatus for applying constant weight to cheese to expel residual whey.

Cheese taster
a tool for removing a sample of cheese to judge its curing.

Cheese toaster
a fork to hold cheese for toasting.

Cherriderry
a cloth similar to streaked calico; used often for clothes of working people.

Chessart
a cheese vat for pressing.

Chesset
a cylindrical container with an open top and a perforated bottom to hold cheese during pressing.

Chest
used alone, generally refers to a box-like piece of furniture with a hinged lid; also found in various combined forms (listed separately).

Chest on chest
a highboy (q.v.) with more or deeper drawers in the lower case and smaller drawers (graduated in size) in the upper case.

Chest over drawer(s)
a chest with an upper section with a lift top and one or more tiers of drawers below.

Cheviot
a breed of sheep.

Chiffon
a thin, light, and soft silk fabric.

Chimney board
= a fender.

Chimney dogs
= andirons.

Chimney glass
a mirror placed over a chimney piece or mantel.

Chimney hook
= pot hook.

Chimney lug
a bar or pole going from one side of a fireplace to the other, on which a kettle is hung over the fire.

Chinchilla cloth
a heavy woolen fabric, napped on one side.

Chintz
a simple, printed cotton fabric.

Chip ax(e)
= broadax.

Chip hat
a hat or bonnet made of wood, palm leaf, straw, etc., split into thin strips and woven together.

Chirurgeon
early form of surgeon.

Chisel
an edged tool of various subtypes used for shaping wood or making various penetrating cuts. Types: framing, wood, mortise, gooseneck = socket-lock, slick = paring, skew, corner.

Chiveret
a woolen fabric.

Chocolate
a pan for making hot chocolate.

Churn
a container in which milk and cream are agitated to make butter.

Cinchona (bark)
the dried bark of any of several species of *Cinchona*, containing several alkaloids including quinine; used medicinally as an anti-fever agent.

Cipher/ciphered
usually indicates something decorated with fancily drawn interwoven letters (often initials).

Circumferentor
an instrument used in navigation and surveying.

Ciselé
a pile fabric with a pattern of blocks of cut and uncut pile.

Cistern
1) a laver; 2) any large vessel for liquids.

Clapse
an adjustable wooden frame for holding a cow's head during milking.

Clarence
a closed, four-wheeled carriage with seats for four inside and a driver's seat outside.

Claret
1) a type of red wine; 2) a color the color of such wine.

Claw
when applied to furniture, usually meaning that the ends of the legs are carved to resemble claws.

Clevis
1) a device consisting of a U-shaped piece of metal with the ends perforated to receive a pin; used on the end of the tongue of a plow, wagon, etc., to

attach it to a draft chain, etc.; 2) = hake, definition #2.

Click reel
a reel with a mechanism that gives an audible click at the completion of each revolution.

Clock reel
a reel with a mechanical counter built in.

Clock-jack
a type of spit which turns automatically.

Closed cupboard
a cupboard with doors.

Closestool
a stool or box to hold a chamber pot.

Closet
a cabinet for various materials; the materials stored therein is usually specified, as in "milk closet."

Clothes press
a receptacle for clothes; e.g. a chest or wardrobe.

Clove
a spice used in cooking; **clove oil** is the oil extracted from clove buds; used in perfumes and medicinally.

Clove water
may refer to oil of clove (see above) or to a liquer flavored with clove (by analogy to anise seed water, q.v.).

Clydesdale
a breed of heavy draft horses.

Coach
a closed, four-wheeled vehicle with two seats facing each other and a fixed top.

Coachee
a closed, four-wheeled, fixed-top vehicle with three forward-facing seats; espe-

cially common in Pennsylvania and New Jersey.

Coal oil
kerosene.

Cobirons
the irons which support a spit.

Cochineal
a red dye made from the dried bodies of the insect *Dactylopius coccus*.

Cock
1) the male of many types of birds, e.g. rooster; 2) a tap or faucet; 3) an iron projection from a plow beam.

Cock blade
probably = cock, definition #3.

Cockade
a rosette, knot, or similar device worn upon a hat as a badge of office, allegiance, or livery service.

Cocked hat
a hat with large stiff flaps turned up to a peaked crown.

Cod (fishing) knives
a group of specialized knives used on cod fishing boats.

Coffer
1) a casket, chest, or trunk, especially one for valuables; 2) a coffin.

Colander
a bowl-like vessel, the bottom of which is perforated; used as a strainer.

Coll
haystack (dialectic Scots).

Cologneware
a term indiscriminately applied to stoneware of German or Dutch origin or style.

Comb-back chair
a type of Windsor chair.

Combination square
see square.

Comfort(er)
1) a woolen scarf worn about the neck;
2) a quilted bed covering.

Comfortier
a little metal brazier in which small coals
could be placed, to be passed around for
pipe lighting.

Commander
= beetle.

Commode
a small closed cupboard with a chest-like
section above, usually with a single
drawer; used to store pitchers, bowls,
shaving tools, etc.

Compass
1) a device for determining direction
relative to the earth's magnetic field; 2)
a device for scribing circles or transfer-
ring measurements.

Conestoga breed
a breed of powerful draft horses.

Conestoga wagon
a heavy freight wagon with a curved
bottom, covered with canvas on bowed
frames; the archetypical "covered
wagon."

Congo
a type of tea.

Console table
a table with a semi-circular top.

Cooper
one who makes containers of wood.
There are two types: wet coopers, who
make containers for liquids; and dry or

slack coopers, who make containers for
dry materials.

Copper
1) a bronze or copper coin; a penny; 2)
sometimes used for something made of
copper, such as a kettle.

Copperas
a yellow dye of ferrous sulphate;
copperas black is a black dye of
logwood with copper as as a mordant.

Coram me
(Latin) "in my presence."

Corded cotton
a fabric of fifty percent linen and fifty
percent cotton with a corded texture.

Cordovan
a soft, fine-grained leather, usually colored.

Corduroy
a cotton fabric with parallel ridges.

Cordwain
cordovan leather.

Cordwainer
a shoemaker.

Corn crib
a house-like structure for storing corn.

Cornelian
sometimes used for carnelian (q.v.).

Corner chair
a chair with a back that extends behind
two full sides.

Cornice
a decorative band put up to conceal the
hooks or rings by which a curtain is hung.

Corriedale
a breed of sheep.

Cosmolabe
a navigational instrument similar to an astrolabe.

Costrel
a bottle of leather, earthenware, or wood, having ears by which it may be hung up.

Cotswold
a breed of sheep.

Cotterel/cotter pole
a trammel or bar from which a pot can be hung over a fire.

Couch
a type of bed.

Coulelace
= cutlass.

Co(u)lter
a knife or disc to split soil ahead of a plowshare.

Counterpane
a coverlet for a bed, originally stitched or woven in squares or figures.

Country linen
= Virginia cloth.

Coupe
(pron. koo-pay´ or koop) a closed, four-wheeled carriage with seating for two people inside and a driver outside.

Court cupboard
a form of cupboard with a closed top and an open base with a shelf.

Coutilas
= cutlass.

Cowl
a large water tub or vessel.

Cradle
1) an infant's bed; 2) a wooden frame-work attached to a scythe to catch grasses as they are cut.

Crane
a metal arm mounted to the side of a fireplace with a hinged joint; used to hold pots over the fire.

Crape
var. of crepe.

Crash(cloth)
a fabric woven from rough yarns, usually cotton or linen.

Cratch
older form of corn crib (q.v.).

Creamware
cream-colored pottery.

Creepers
low, small andirons.

Crepe
any fabric which remains permanently wrinkled.

Cresset
an iron vessel or basket for holding burning oil, pitchy wood, etc., and mounted as a torch or suspended as a lantern.

Cretonne
a heavy cotton or linen fabric, printed; used for upholstery.

Crewel
worsted yarn, slackly twisted; used usually for embroidery, but also for fringes, laces, etc.

Crocus
a coarse cloth.

Crome/cromb
a tool with three down-turned tines for raking manure from a muck cart (q.v.).

Crook
= pot hook.

Crook chain
a chain with a hook, affixed to a fireplace, from which a pot is hung.

Crooked lane ware
tinware.

Cross reel
a hand reel in which the end pieces are not only at right angles to the staff, but also to each other.

Cross-staff
a navigational instrument for determining the azimuth of the sun.

Crow
1) a bar or iron with a beak, crook, or two claws; used to raise or move heavy weights; 2) a grapnel; 3) a type of door knocker.

Crown
a British silver coin worth five shillings; also as a gold coin.

Crown glass
window glass blown and whirled into a disc, in the center of which is a knot called the bull's eye; it is cut into panes.

Croze
a tool for cutting the groove near the end of each stave of a barrel into which the barrelhead is inserted.

Cruel
var. of crewel.

Cruet
a bottle or vessel for holding vinegar, oil, pepper, etc., at the table.

Cruiskin
= cruse.

Crumbcloth
1) a cloth to lay on or under a dining table to catch crumbs; 2) a heavy damask, suitable for use in embroidery.

Crupper
(also pron. as if cruper) a leather strap passing under a horse's tail and buckled to the saddle to keep it from slipping.

Cruse
a pot-shaped vessel with a spout and handle.

Crusekyn
= cruse.

Crusie
= cresset.

Cruskin
= cruse.

Cultivator
a tool for opening soil; it works deeper than a harrow.

Curb
a chain used to check an unruly animal.

Curd breaker
a long-handled device with several blades for cutting the curd during cheese making.

Curd knife
a knife with a very long blade; used for cutting curd during cheese making.

Curricle
a two-wheeled chaise drawn by two horses abreast.

Currier
1) one who curries and dresses leather after it is tanned; 2) one who curries horses.

Curtle axe
= cutlass.

Cut
a unit of measure for linen yarn = 300 yards.

Cutilax
= cutlass.

Cutlace
= cutlass.

Cutlash
= cutlass.

Cutlass
a short single-edged sword, sometimes with a straight blade, sometimes with a curved blade.

Cutter
1) a small sleigh for one or two persons; 2) a broad, square-sterned boat for carrying stores or passengers to and from a warship; 3) a fore-and-aft rigged ship with a mainmast and a jib and forestay-sail.

Cutting box
as a tool, most probably a mitre box.

Cylinder (front) desk
a desk with a one-piece lid or cover resembling a longitudinal section of a cylinder.

Cypher
var. of cipher.

Cypress
applied to furniture, usually means the wood rather than the country.

Dader
= twibel or twivel.

Daffy's Elixir (Salutis)
a patent medicine (q.v.).

Dalby's Carminative
a patent medicine (q.v.).

Damask
a fine silk or linen fabric.

Damnified
damaged.

Danzik
1) of cloth, linen; 2) of spiritous liquor, brandy.

Davis' quadrant
= back-staff.

Daybed
essentially a long chair with six or eight legs and usually with a canted back.

Deal
1) pine or fir wood; loosely, any plain, unfinished wood; 2) a unit of timber measurement, originally a board 3 inches thick, 9 inches wide, and 12 feet long ("**standard deal**"); **whole deal**, 1 1/4 inches thick; **slit deal**, 5/8 inches thick; **five-cut stuff**, 1/2 inch or less thick; **deal ends**, any piece less than six feet long; later, a size varies with locality; 3) a rare Dutch wine.

Delaine
a light cloth of wool or wool and cotton.

Delft(ware)
(note: the "t" is very frequently omitted) tin-glazed earthenware originally from Holland.

Demi-castor
= caster.

Demijohn
a narrow-necked bottle of glass or stoneware, holding one to ten gallons, enclosed in wickerwork and having one or two handles.

Denim
a coarse cotton fabric.

Desk box
= writing box.

Dessert knife, fork, spoon, plate
a knife, fork, spoon, or plate for use with desserts and smaller than regular tableware.

Diaper
any fabric decorated all over with small patterns.

Dibble
a small spade, usually used in planting.

Dimety
a cotton fabric which was quite stout through the 19th century; only in the 20th century did it become sheer.

Dimity
a fine, corded cotton fabric.

Dip hook
a shepherd's staff with a hook or combination of hooks on the end for handling sheep.

Diptych dial
a form of portable sundial.

Distaff
the staff for holding the bunch of flax, tow, or wool from which the thread is drawn in spinning by hand or with a wheel.

Ditch hoe
probably a mattock.

Ditto
"the same as written above;" abbrev. Do, do, D°.

Dividers
a two-pronged, hinged instrument for measuring map scales and marking off distances on maps; sometimes with a screw gear to regulate the distance they are open.

Dobra
a Portuguese gold goin, worth about £3/ 18/5; also called a joe or a double johannes.

Dock(ing) iron
a tool for clipping an animal's tail; usually used on horses and sheep.

Dog
1) a block of iron; 2) fireplace andirons; 3) a tool of various types to clamp down wood for milling, hewing, sawing, etc.; 4) a clamp for holding logs together to form a raft.

Dog dollar
= lion dollar.

Dog lock
a type of flintlock.

Dolly (stick)
a wooden instrument used to beat or stir clothes in a tub as part of washing.

Dolly tub
a wash tub used in conjunction with a dolly stick.

Dornix
a heavy cloth of silk, wool, or silk and wool.

Dorset horn
a breed of sheep.

Dory
a flat-bottomed boat with high flaring sides; used as a fishing boat in New England.

Double johannes/joe
= dobra.

Doublet
a close-fitting garment for men, with or without sleeves, covering the body from the neck to the waist or a little below.

Dough box table
essentially a dough trough (usually with splayed sides) that has legs attached (again, usually splayed) and a single or multiple board top.

Dough trough
an oblong container used for mixing and kneading dough.

Dovetail
in combinations, indicates a trapizoidal shape.

Dower chest
a type of chest over drawers, often brightly painted or decorated with inlays.

Dowlas
a linen cloth made completely of long flax strands.

Dozen
1) a quantity of twelve; 2) a coarse woolen cloth.

Drab
a thick woolen cloth of dull brownish-yellow color; usually used for overcoats.

Draft
1) applied to animals, indicates that they could pull heavy loads; 2) a map.

Dram
a liquid measure = 1/8 oz.

Draught
an older spelling of draft.

Draw
sometimes used for drawer.

Draw hoe
a hook-shaped hoe with the cutting edge inside the hook so it cuts when pulled toward the user.

Drawboy
1) a part of a loom; 2) a type of cloth.

Drawers
an undergarment worn on the lower body and legs.

Drawknife/drawing knife
an edged tool with a handle on each end; designed to be used by drawing it over the wood toward the user.

Dray
1) a kind of sledge or cart without wheels; 2) a strong, low, usually two-wheeled cart or wagon for carrying heavy goods; 3) loosely, any heavy wagon for hauling goods.

Dreadnought/dreadnaught
= fearnought.

Dredger
var. of drudger.

Dressing glass
a mirror swung in a frame designed to be set on, not fastened to, a chest of drawers or table.

Dressing table
a table with a rectangular top, a backboard, one or more tiers of drawers below, and sometimes one or more tiers of small drawers on the back of the top.

Drill(ing)
a twilled linen fabric.

Drinking tobacco
smoking tobacco.

Drudger
a box from which flour is thrown at roast meat.

Drugg stuff
a woolen cloth used for heavy cloaks; = drugget, definition #1.

Drugget
1) a type of woolen or mixed stuff for

clothing; 2) a coarse cloth used as a lining or protective covering for carpets or furniture; 3) a rug with a cotton warp and wool filling.

Dry sink
a low closed cupboard with a shallow well above it.

Dryfatt
a fatt (q.v.) to hold dry commodities.

Ducape
a heavy corded silk fabric.

Ducat
a gold coin worth about 9/5; also silver coin worth about half the gold ducat.

Duck
a strong, heavy linen fabric.

Duck's foot pistol
a box or flintlock with four to seven barrels fitted to a single breechblock.

Duffel/duffield
a coarse woolen cloth with a thick nap.

Dun
any of several colors varying from red to yellow.

Dung fork
a tined tool used for moving manure or working it into the soil.

Dunghill fowl
the common domestic fowl.

Duroc
a breed of hog.

Duroc-Jersey
a breed of hog.

Durrie/durry
a thick cotton cloth.

Dutch belted
a breed of dairy cattle.

Dutch cupboard
a type of closed cupboard.

Dutch drops
a patent medicine consisting of oil of turpentine, tincture of guaiacum, spirit of miter, oil of amber, and oil of cloves.

Dutch gold
= Dutch metal.

Dutch metal
tombac (q.v.), esp. in the form of a foil.

Dutch oven
a tub-shaped kettle with small legs on the base and a tight-fitting lid; surrounded and covered with hot coals for baking.

Ear knot
probably part of a wig.

Earbob
an earring.

Eardrop
an earring.

Earthenware
anything made by a potter.

Elbow chair
a chair with upholstered arms.

Elixir Salutis
a patent medicine (q.v.).

Ell
a unit of measure = forty-five inches.

English lock
a type of flintlock

Entry
in New England, a small room just inside the front door; in the South, it often

ran the entire depth of the house and had a back door at the other end.

Epee
a slim-bladed sword, similar to a rapier, used for fencing.

Epergne
(pron. a-pern´) a centerpiece for table decoration, usually consisting of several grouped dishes or receptacles.

Ephemeris
(pl. Ephermerides) a book of computed positions for celestial bodies for use in navigational calculations.

Equinoctial ring
a navigational instrument.

Equipage
1) the furniture (q.v.) or supplies necessary to something (e.g. a ship, an army, a single soldier; 2) a set or collection of articles for personal use (e.g. in dressing); also a case to hold such articles; 3) a carriage of state or for pleasure, with all the horses, liverymen, etc., that accompany it.

Escutcheon
an ornamental shield around a keyhole.

Essence of Peppermint
a patent medicine (q.v.).

Estamine
a cloth, a type of serge.

E'toffe du pays
a heavy homespun cloth of 100 percent wool.

Everlasting
hard-wearing woolens resembling serge.

Evil
a three-tined tool used for spreading manure on fields.

Ewe
a female sheep.

Ewer
a widemouthed pitcher or jug.

Fag(g)ot
a bundle of anything but usually of sticks.

Faggot fork
a two-tined fork with a long handle; used to handle faggots in a fireplace or oven.

Faïence
a decorative earthenware, as opposed to tableware, originally applied to ware made in France.

Falchion
a short, single-edged sword with a broad, heavy blade.

Fall-front desk
a desk, the top section of which has a hinged vertical lid that falls forward to form a writing surface.

Fancy chair
almost any paint-decorated Sheraton chair.

Farm table
= work table.

Farthingale
a hoop skirt or hoop petticoat, or a frame or hoops (usually whalebone) used to extend the petticoat.

Fat/fatt(e)
a vat, cask, barrel, or box.

Fathom
a measure of length (usually of cables, cordage, nets, etc.) containing five to six feet; originally the space between a man's outstretched arms, and probably measured that way in making inventories.

Fearnaught
= fearnought.

Fearnothing
= fearnought.

Fearnought
a stout woolen cloth of great thickness; a warm garment made from such cloth.

Felt
a fabric made by pressing fibers together under moist heat.

Fender
a low metal frame, often ornate, placed before a fireplace.

Ferret(ing)/ferrit(ing)
a kind of narrow tape, originally of silk but also of cotton or wool.

Fetters
= hopple.

Fiddle-back chair
a chair in which the back rest is fiddle-shaped.

Field bed
1) a portable bed, usually folding for use in the field; 2) a four-post bed of moderate height with a canopy supported on a strongly arched frame.

Filet
a type of lace or net with a square mesh.

Filliting
probably derived from **fillet**, a band worn about the hair; hence, material similar to ribbon suitable for use as a fillet.

Filly
a female colt or young mare.

Filter
a strainer or searce.

Fire-back/fire-plate
a large plate of iron, often ornate, placed behind the fire in a fireplace to protect the masonry.

Fire-bucket
a bucket, usually of leather, kept by individuals for use collectively when fighting fires.

Firedogs
andirons.

Firelock
flintlock.

Fire-pike
a fireplace poker.

Fire-plate
a fire-back.

Fireslice
A fireplace shovel.

Firkin
a unit of measure = 8 gallons or 6 1/2 pounds.

Firmer
a type of chisel or gouge about one foot long and usually designed to be driven with a mallet.

Fish-kettle
an oblong cauldron.

Flagon
a drinking vessel with a narrow mouth.

Flail
a hand tool used to strike grain to separate seed from chaff.

Flake white
a type of white lead.

Flanders(ware)
stoneware.

Flannel
a light, napped woolen cloth.

Flannelette
imitation flannel made of cotton.

Flasket
1) a shallow basket; 2) a shallow oval tub; 3) a small flask.

Flat
a boat with a flat bottom and boarded-over ends; used for freight and ferrying.

Flatiron
an iron with a flat smooth surface for ironing clothes; the same name was used for old types which required an external heat source as well as later types heated electrically.

Flax wheel
a small type of spinning wheel; used to make flax thread.

Fleam
a medical instrument for letting blood.

Fleeter
a device for skimming cream off milk.

Fleeting-dish
a skimming bowl.

Flesh fork
an iron prong to lift meat from the pot.

Flesh hook
a hook to lift meat from a pot.

Fleshing knife
a two-handled, convex, blunt-edged knife for scraping the flesh side of a hide in curing.

Flint glass
a heavy brilliant glass containing lead; crystal glass.

Flintlock
technically the firing mechanism of a musket, rifle, etc., in which the priming powder is ignited by a spark from flint and steel; often used to refer to the entire gun having such a mechanism.

Flip
a spiced and sweetened drink of ale, beer, or cider and another liquor such as rum, sometimes containing egg.

Flip dog
a straight or hooked piece of iron, often with a spoon-shaped tip, heated in a fire and thrust into drinks (originally flip) to give them a burnt taste.

Flock
1) woolen or cotton refuse, old rags, etc., reduced by machinery and used as stuffing; 2) a bed stuffed with flock (sense 1).

Flocket
a loose, long-sleeved garment.

Floor cloth
an oil cloth for floors.

Florameda
probably a flowered or figured cloth.

Florence
1) money: a gold florin; 2) a woolen cloth; 3) a silk dress material; a thin taffeta, sometimes corded; 4) a red wine; 5) herb: sweet fennel.

Floss
a soft, lustrous silk thread, often used in embroidery.

Fodder
dried grasses stored as animal food for the winter.

Foot adz
an adz (q.v.) with a straight, unlipped blade.

Footman
= trivet.

Foot-mantle
safeguard.

Forage harvester
a machine to cut and shred grass for silage.

Forestaff
= cross-staff.

Form
a long, backless seat.

Foulard
a light, printed fabric of silk (or imitation of cotton).

Fowler/fowling piece
a type of musket with a very long barrel; later also used of shotguns

French blue
= ultramarine (snythetic).

French Canadian
applied to animals, a breed of dairy cattle.

Friar's cloth
a fabric woven in basket weave.

Frieze
a heavy woolen cloth with uncut nap.

Frigate
originally a light seagoing vessel with both sails and oars; later used only of warships.

Fringe loom
a type of small loom used for weaving decorative fringes.

Frock
1) a man's coat, usually double-breasted and usually reaching to the knees; 2) a gown or dress; originally a child's or girl's dress, but later used more generally.

Frocking
a coarse linen fabric, often striped.

Froe/frow
a wedge-shaped cleaving tool used for cutting slabs of wood for use as shingles.

Frog
1) a loop attached to the belt to hold a sword; 2) an ornamental braiding on a coat or dress, often in loops and with a fastening for a button.

Frow
= froe.

Fulham jug
a drinking vessel of heavy ceramic material.

Fulham(ware)
a popular term for a wide range of pottery, tavern tankards, and bottles made in London.

Furlong
a unit of measure = 660 feet.

Furnishings
referring to a person, personal items such as clothes, jewelry, toilet articles, etc.

Furniture
1) besides the usual meaning of chairs, tables, etc., also used for a set of articles that constitute necessary appendages to something; 2) as an adjective, can mean decorative or for embellishment or show.

Furrow press
a roller to make furrows for seed.

Fusil
a light (and during the 1700' musket.

Fustian
a heavy-twilled fabric of 40 percent linen and 60 percent cotton, softly brushed on one side; later used of a class of cut pile fabrics like velveteen.

Fustic
a yellow dye made from the wood of *Chlorophora tinctoria*; also used of other dyewoods.

Gall
= nutgall.

Galley ware
= delftware.

Gallipot
a small vessel; used especially for medicines.

Gallnut
= nutgall.

Galloon
a cotton or silk braid used for trimming clothes.

Galloway
1) a breed of small, hardy horses; 2) a hardy breed of medium-sized, hornless beef cattle.

Gallows-balke
a chimney lug.

Gallows-crook
a pot hook.

Gallus frame
a type of small loom.

Gambrel
a crooked stick or iron used by butchers to suspend slaughtered animals.

Garlix
probably a variety of gulix.

Garnet
a type of hinge with an upright bar and a horizontal strap.

Garret
technically the story of a house under the roof and above the second floor, but seems to have been used loosely as any area under the slope of the roof and above another room.

Garter loom
a type of small loom.

Gateleg table
a leafed table with six to eight legs; one leg on each side swings out to support a leaf.

Gauze
a very thin silk cloth.

Gavel
a hook for pulling cut grain together.

Gelding
a castrated male horse.

Gemma's ring
a sunclock used for navigation.

Gentlewoman
besides meaning a woman of high station, it can mean one who attends a person of high station; this was seen in only one inventory and probably meant a female servant (indentured) who served as a chambermaid.

Georgette
a light silk fabrice, twisted to give the appearance of silk.

German wheel
a type of flax wheel.

Gib-croke/gib-crook
a pot hook.

Gig
1) a name commonly applied to the chaise during the 19th century; 2) a two- or three-pronged spearhead with barbed points for catching fish, frogs, etc.

Gigger
variety of jigger.

Gill
a liquid measure = 1/4 pint.

Gilt
gilded.

Gimlet
a small tool with a screw point, grooved shank, and cross handle; used for boring holes.

Gimlin
a salting tub.

Gimp
a narrow ornamental fabric of silk, wool, or cotton, often with a metal wire or cord running through it; used as trimming for dresses, furniture, etc.

Gingham
a checked or striped cotton dress fabric.

Ginseng
the aromatic root of *Panax schinseng* or *P. quinquefolium*; used as a medicinal herb.

Gipse
a wooden spice or sugar mortar.

Girandole
1) an ornamental branched candleholder; 2) a convex mirror in a richly ornamented circular frame with two or more sconces attached; 3) a kind of earring, especially one with small stones grouped around a larger one.

Girdle
basically anything that encircles the waist, as 1) a belt; 2) a woman's garment with laces encircling the body between hips and bust; worn under or over other clothes.

Girth
1) a piece of harness which circles the animal's body to hold on a saddle, etc.; 2) a girdle (also in the sense of armor).

Giskin
a leather drinking vessel.

Gloster
phonetic spelling Gloucester.

Gloucester cheese
(pronounced Gloster) a type of pressed cheese.

Glut
= wedge.

Goad
a measure of cotton cloth = 1 1/2 yards.

Gocart
1) a framework moving on casters to support children learning to walk; 2) a baby carriage; 3) a handcart; 4) a kind of light carriage.

Godfrey's General Cordial
a patent medicine (q.v.).

Goglet
a long-necked water vessel, usually of porous earthenware for cooling water by evaporation.

Goloe-shoes
= pattens.

Gondola
1) a heavy, flat-bottomed boat, often with a single sail; 2) a ship's boat.

Goosewing
a type of broadaxe.

Gorget
1) a crescent-shaped piece of metal worn suspended from the neck of an officer (a vestigial form of armor); 2) a collar; 3) a kind of covering for the neck and breast (worn by women); 4) a neck ornament.

Gouge
a tool similar to a chisel but with a rounded blade.

Graffito
var. of sgraffito.

Granite cloth
a wool cloth with a rough texture.

Graphometer
a surveying instrument for measuring angles.

Grapnel
a multi-tined hook used for grasping and hauling; today more commonly called a grappling hook.

Grapple
1) a device, usually a hook, by which something can be grabbed or held; 2) a bent hook for digging.

Grappling
as a noun, a grapple.

Grate
a fireplace; the word is often used to qualify other nouns, as in "grate shovel."

Graybeard
= bellarmine.

Great coat
a heavy overcoat.

Great wheel
a type of spinning wheel with a very large wheel.

Gridiron
a metal device, usually made up of a series of parallel bars, with legs; used to support pots for cooking over an open fire.

Grog
an unsweetened mixture or a liquor (originally rum) and water.

Grograine
a coarse fabric of silk or mohair and wool (sometimes mixed with silk).

Grogram
var. of grograine.

Groping hoe
a heavy hoe, similar to a mattock, used for breaking ground.

Gross
a unit of quantity = 144.

Grub(bing) hoe
= groping hoe.

Gudgeon
a metal pivot, fixed in the end of a wooden shaft (usually an axle).

Guernsey
a breed of dairy cattle.

Gugget
var. of goglet.

Guinea
a British gold coin worth twenty-one shillings (after 1717; earlier the value varied slightly).

Gulix
a fine white linen.

Gum
a vessel or bin made from a hollowed log.

Gum arabic
the gum from several species of acacia; used to make adhesives, inks, and confections, also in textile printing and pharmacy.

Gum sandarac
see sandarac.

Gun
a nebulous term that may mean a musket, a rifle, or a cannon. It is rarely used for pistol.

Gundalow
var. of gondola.

Gunny
= burlap.

Gunter's scale
a wooden or brass ruler one to two feet long, engraved with geometric and trigonometric scales for navigation and surveying.

Gurglet
var. of goglet.

Gyle
1) the beer produced at one brewing; 2) a vat in which beer is fermented; 3) wort in an incipient state of fermentation; added to a stout or ale.

Hackel
= hetchell.

Hadley quadrant/octant
a navigational instrument similar to a sextant.

Hair
in combined forms, can refer to "for the hair" or "made of hair," as in haircloth or hair sifter.

Hair pencil
a paint brush.

Haircloth
a fabric into which horse hair has been woven.

Hake
1) a pot hook; 2) an attachment for a plow.

Half crown
a British silver coin worth 2/6.

Half joe
= johannes.

Hall
the living room and kitchen of a one-room 17th-century house. When there was a separate kitchen, the name was still retained. It was not a passageway as today.

Hame
one of two curved pieces of wood or metal to which the traces are fastened in a harness for heavy draft animals.

Hammel
a type of cloth; may be a var. of stammel.

Hammer
a metal tool used for pounding. Wooden hammers were usually called mallets (q.v.). Types: cooper's, veneer, claw, cobbler's.

Hammer cloth
an ornamental cloth hung over the driver's seat or box of a coach.

Hammer mill
a mill working with a pounding action.

Hampshire down
a breed of sheep.

Hand reel
a device, usually of wood, consisting of three pieces put together in the form of an "I"; used to make skeins of yarn or thread of constant length.

Handbarrow
a device, similar in shape to a ladder, carried by two people like a stretcher; used to carry cargo.

Hand-glass
a portable framework of iron, wood, etc., glazed with numerous panes of glass; used to protect seedlings.

Handiron
1) a small anvil for light work, usually with a tang to fit in a hole in a bench; 2) var. of andiron.

Handscrew
1) a tool like a gimlet; 2) a tool for tightening bed cords; 3) a tool for twisting grasses to be used in binding stalks of grains.

Hanger
a short, lightweight, single-edged sword with a slightly curved blade.

Harness
1) a group of heddles on a loom; 2) a set of straps by which an animal is bound to a load; the components of standard harness include: reins, overcheck rein, checkhook, terret, crownpiece, front, blind, facepiece, cheekpiece, throatlatch, neck strap, breast band/collar, saddle, bellyband, breeching, crupper, hip strap, trace, billet, hame, chokestrap, neck yoke, breeching stay, lazy strap. Not every harness rig contains all of the above.

Harness cask
a food storage cask for shipboard use.

Harpoon
a barbed spear with a length of rope attached; used in whaling.

Harquebus
= arquebus.

Har(r)ateen
a fabric of wool or hair; used for hangings, furniture, etc.

Harrow
a cultivation implement, originally with tines, for breaking up and smoothing soil; also occurs as **disc harrow**, which has discs rather than tines.

Hartshorn
1) the antler of a deer; 2) ammonium carbonate; 3) a type of plantain.

Harvest table
usually a very long dining table with two drop leaves.

Hasp
1) any of various clasps or fastenings, especially a hinged metal strap passed over a staple and secured with a pin; 2) a spindle for winding yarn; 3) a skein or hank of yarn.

Hatchel
= hetchel.

Hatchet
an edged tool, originally a one-handed broadax; used for shaping wood. Later various types were developed as multipurpose tools: lathering hatchet, shingling hatchet, cooper's hatchet.

Hay bond twister
a tool for making straw rope to bind sheaves.

Hay ladder
a ladder used to climb haystacks.

Hay sweep
a pronged scoop for collecting hay.

Hayfork
= pitchfork.

Hayknife
an edged tool similar to a sickle but edged on the opposite side of the blade; used to cut hay out of haystacks.

Hayrick
a haystack.

Head cloth
a cloth forming a screen for the head of a bed or of a person.

Heckel
= hetchel.

Heddle
a part of a loom consisting of a series of metal wire "eyes" through which some of the warp threads pass; more than one is used, allowing one group of warp threads to be separated from others to form patterns during weaving.

Heddle and harness maker/jig
a piece of equipment for constructing heddle and their harness for use on a loom.

Heffer
phonetic spelling of heifer.

Heifer
(pron. hef´fer) a young cow; a cow that has not had a calf.

Hemp
a vegetable fiber similar to flax but coarser; most often used for rope but also in coarse fabric.

Hen-basket
= pannier 2).

Hereford
a breed of beef cattle.

Hessians
coarse cloth of hemp or jute.

Hetchel
a narrow board with a group of long, headless spikes set close together protruding from it; used to strip the fibers from flax stems.

High chest
= highboy.

Highboy
basically a chest of drawers supported on another chest of drawers with long legs.

Hill's Balsom of Honey
a patent medicine (q.v.).

Hitchcock chair
= fancy chair.

Hobble
= hopple.

Hock
originally Hockheimer, a variety of Rhein wine; later, any white wine.

Hock bond
probably = hopple.

Hog's fat
lard.

Hogshead
1) a large cask or barrel; 2) a unit of liquid measure = about sixty-three gallons (but varies).

Holland
applied to cloth, a heavy, usually coarse fabric.

Holland china
= delftware.

Hollow shave
a drawknife with a curved blade; used for hollowing wood.

Hollow-ware
a generic term for cast-iron vessels; e.g., pots, pans, skillets; cf. sadware.

Holstein
a breed of dairy cattle.

Hominy
a dry maize product made by removing the hull and breaking the kernel into coarse particles; originally the grinding was done with a large wooden mortar and pestle.

Hoof pick
a pointed tool for cleaning materials from horses' hooves.

Hook
1) any of several types of reaping hooks; usually qualified as rice hook, indigo hook, etc.; 2) a fishing hook.

Hookabag
older spelling of huckaback.

Hoop-skirt rocker
a rocking chair in which the arms do not extend completely to the front of the seat.

Hooper's (Female) Pills
a patent medicine (q.v.).

Hopple
a fetter for grazing horses or cattle or to control a horse's gait.

Hops
the dried ripe cones of the female flowers of a climbing vine; used medicinally and in beer and ale.

Hornbook
a kind of child's primer consisting of a piece of parchment or paper on which are the alphabet and other rudiments, protected by a piece of transparent horn; the whole is then mounted on a wooden board.

Horse
any of various types of bench-like apparatus; used to hold materials being worked on.

Horse pistol
a large pistol, originally designed to be carried in a scabbard on a saddle.

Hotwell water
mineral water.

Howel
a cooper's smoothing and chamfering tool; used especially for smoothing the insides of casks.

Huck
= huckaback.

Huckaback
a strong fabric of linen or linen and cotton with an uneven surface, sometimes figured.

Hummeller
see barley hummeller.

Hunting bag
a pouch similar to a cartridge box but used by civilians and militiamen.

Hutch
a storage box built into a piece of furniture.

Hutch table
a box supported on legs, above which is a hinged table top which, when raised, can serve as a backrest or, when lowered, as a table.

Hyson
a type of green tea from China.

Idle-back
= pot hook rachette.

Imari
a style of porcelain decoration originally from Japan, but later applied indescriminately to any Oriental pattern.

Imperial
a type of tea.

Imprimis
(Latin) "first of all."

Inclinometer
a sensitive and accurate instrument for measuring the force and direction of magnetic fields.

Indenture
1) a mutual agreement between two or more parties; 2) a specific case of such an agreement in which one person is bound into service to another for a fixed period of time in return for the second person's providing a service for the first. The service was often paying the indenturee's fare to America, but it could also be the providing of training in a craft (also called apprenticeship). In inventories a value is often given for an indentured servant; this valuation reflects the amount of time left to be served in the contract. See also page 58.

Indian
referring to crops or food, a type of corn.

Indian red
a yellowish-red pigment made by calcining iron salts; originally a ferruginous earth from the Persian Gulf, hence it is also called Persian red.

Indico
var. of indigo.

Indigo
1) any of several plants, esp. *Indigofera* sp., used to produce a blue dye; 2) the dye obtained from these plants; 3) the color indigo blue.

Ingrain carpet
a carpet made of wool dyed before manufacture. It is reversible, a similar design but with reversed colors appearing on each side.

Ink powder
a dry form of writing ink to be mixed with water for use.

Inkhorn
a small bottle for holding ink; originally made of horn, but later of other materials.

Inkle
a type of linen tape or braid.

Iron
used in combination with the names of various foods, a device for holding that food while it is cooked or toasted.

Iron rubber
a sailmaker's tool.
Iron square
see square.

Irondogs
usually = firedogs.

Ironmongery
1) a factory where iron is made; 2) articles made of iron.

Ironstone (china)
a hard white pottery made in England.

Isinglass
1) a whitish, semi-transparent form of gelatin; used in making jellies, glue, etc.; 2) mica, especially in thin, transparent sheets.

Ivory teeth
usually refers to whale teeth rather than a dental prosthetic.

Jack
1) an instrument to turn spits; 2) a cup made of waxed leather; 3) a support to saw on; 4) a tool for removing boots.

Jacob's staff
= cross-staff.

Jaconet
a soft muslin cloth.

Jade
1) a gemstone, commonly green but sometimes whitish, often carved and polished; 2) an old, worn-out horse.

Jam cupboard
= jelly cupboard.

Jam pike
a wooden pole with a pointed metal head; used for moving floating logs.

Jamaica spirits
rum.

Jane
a strong fabric of fifty percent linen and fifty percent cotton; used for underwear and outerwear.

Jannock
a leavened oatmeal bread; the word is often found in combinations like jannock tub—a tub for mixing jannock ingredients.

Japan
a varnish with a hard, brilliant surface; laquer. Often found as **japanned**—treated or coated with japan.

Jelly cupboard
usually a one-piece closed cupboard with one or two doors and one or two drawers above them.

Jerkin
a jacket or short coat; a close waistcoat.

Jersey
a breed of dairy cattle.

Jesuit ring
a finger ring, usually of brass, with large and irregularly shaped bezels, on which was an inscription or initials; often used as trade goods.

Jesuit's bark
= cinchona.

Jigger/gigger
a draw knife with a blade straight on one end and hollow on the other.

Jill
var. of gill.

Jockey
1) a thin cap with a long visor; 2) a great coat, especially one of broadcloth with wide sleeves.

Joe
= dobra.

Johannes
a Portuguese gold coin, worth about 36/2 1/2; usually called a half-joe.

Joint stool
a small stool with the parts held together by pegged mortise and tenon joints.

Jointer
1) a mason's tool for pointing joints; 2) a tool for marking out joints; 3) a type of plane; 4) a part of a plow; 5) a cabinet maker.

Kas
a piece of furniture with a large, wardrobe-like upper section, with or without shelves, over one to three drawers.

Keelboat
a large, flat-bottomed boat used on rivers.

Keeler
a shallow wooden tub.

Keelfat
a tub for cooling liquids.

Keeping room
= a hall.

Keeve
a vat or tub, as a brewer's mash tub, a bleaching kier or a washing tub used in treating ores.

Kentine/kenting
a type of cloth.

Kercher
var. of kerchief.

Kersey
a coarse, ribbed, light woolen cloth.

Ketch
a two-masted, fore-and-aft rigged sailing vessel.

Kettle-tilter
see pot hook, rachette.

Kibble
a wooden bucket used to draw water from a well.

Kier
a large vat in which textile goods are boiled, bleached, etc.

Kilderkin
a cask one-half or even one-quarter the size of a common barrel; usually = eighteen gallons or two firkins.

King's yellow
= orpiment.

Kipe
a basket, often for measuring.

Kitchen
1) a room or a separate building used for cooking; 2) a tin roasting oven for use in a fireplace.

Kitt-katt
a unit of measure = 36" x 28".

Knee buckle
a buckle to secure breeches at the knee.

Kneehole desk
a flat-topped desk, usually with two tiers of several drawers flanking an opening for the user's knees.

Lac
a resinous substance from an insect (*Tachardia lacca*). It is known by various names, depending on the degree and type of processing; e. g. **seed-lac, stick-lac, button-lac**, etc.; used in sealing wax, lacquer, etc.

Ladder-back chair
a chair, usually in the Chippendale style, with a back that has horizontal slats, hence making it look like a ladder; sometimes used as equivalent to slat-back chair.

Lade-gorn
a large piggin.

Lake
a purplish-red pigment prepared from lac or cochineal.

Lambeth(ware)
a type of delftware.

Lamb(s)kin
a woolen or cotton fabric imitating lambskin fur.

Lamé
any fabric, but often silk, containing threads of flat metal.

Lamp
a generic term for any container that could hold a wick suspended in a flammable material (e.g. grease, oil, kerosene) to produce light; in earlier forms the flame was open: there was no chimney.

Lampblack
a fine, bulky, black soot used in paints, varnishes, and ink.

Lancet
a medical instrument for lancing infections and letting blood.

Landau
a four-wheeled, covered vehicle with a top divided into two sections, the back section of which can be let down or thrown back while the front section can be removed or left stationary.

Lanthorn
var. of lantern.

Lap loom
a small loom, consisting of a single piece of wood with holes and slits cut into it; designed to be held between the knees for making tapes, etc.

Lap robe
usually a blanket or fur spread over the lap for warmth, especially in sleighs and carriages.

Larder
a room where meat and other uncooked foods are kept.

Last
1) any of a varied group or units of measure, the volume and nature of which depend on what is being measured; e.g., length (lumber), tonnage (shipping), weight (grains), volume (cargo), number (hides); 2) a wooden or metal block shaped like a foot, over which shoes are made.

Latten
a type of brass or brass alloy hammered into sheets; later also used for sheet iron and galvanized iron.

Lattenware
utensils made of latten.

Laudanum
a sedative medication based on opium.

Laundry bat
a wooden paddle used for stirring clothes during washing.

Lavender & Hungary Water
a patent medicine (q.v.).

Laver
a bowl for washing.

Lawn
a thin cotton fabric.

Lazy-back
see pot hook, rachette.

Leach
1) a tub in which tanbark is steeped in water to make tan liquor for tanning hides; 2) a barrel for making lye from ashes.

Leeds(ware)
cream-colored earthenware from Staffordshire and elsewhere.

Leicester
(pron. Les´ter) a breed of sheep.

Lester
phonetic spelling of Leicester.

Library table
basically a larger version of the tavern table.

Lift-top (commode)
= commode.

Lighter
a barge used in unloading ships that cannot be docked.

Lignum vitae
a type of hard wood.

Limbeck
alembic.

Limner
one who draws or paints, especially an illustrator of books.

Lincoln
a breed of sheep.

Linen
cloth made from flax; of various types and grades.

Linen press
a piece of furniture with a closed cupboard upper section (with shelves) and three to five drawers below.

Linsey-woolsey
a strong, durable, and warm cloth made of linen and wool.

Lion dollar
a silver Dutch coin, worth about the same as a Spanish milled dollar; also called a dog dollar.

Littler's blue
a cobalt-colored lead glaze used on pottery.

Livery
1) the attire befitting a certain occupation or station; 2) a low grade of wool; 3) of horses, the feeding, stabling, and care thereof.

Loaf sugar
= sugar loaf.

Locker
a small cupboard fitted into the interior of a desk.

Lockerum
a linen fabric

Lockyer's Pills
a patent medicine (q.v.).

Log
a device for measuring a ship's speed.

Log(book)
a journal kept by ship's captains.

Loggerhead
= flip dog.

Logwood
a reddish-blue dye made from the heartwood of the tree *Haematoxylon campechianum*.

Longcloth
a light, soft cotton fabric.

Long-short
a long, loose, shapeless jacket or smock, usually made of striped frocking.

Looking glass
a mirror.

Loop
a fold of cord or ribbon through which a button or hook is passed, acting as a button hole; often an ornament on military clothing.

Losset
a trencher.

Lot
a number of associated things taken collectively; **not** used to mean "a large number of."

Lottery
refers to something allotted, either purposefully or by chance.

Loud hailer
a metal megaphone used on ships.

Lowboy
a piece of furniture like the bottom part of a highboy.

Low-post bed
= under-eaves bed.

Lug pole/stick
= chimney lug.

Lugger
a partially decked fishing boat with a single mast.

Lumber
besides the usual meaning of prepared wood, it can also mean old or refuse household items.

Lungee/lungi
a long cloth worn as a scarf.

Luster/lustre
a light-giving object, usually a chandelier.

Lustring
a plain, stout, lustrous silk cloth used for dresses and ribbon.

Lutestring
a corruption of lustring.

Machete
a large swinging knife.

Machin
perhaps a var. of mackinboy; also found as a common misspelling of machine.

Mackinaw
a thick wool or wool and cotton fabric; also a coat made of such materials.

Mackinboy/mackenboy
a root used as a purgative.

Madder
a red dye made from the ground roots of *Rubia tinctorum*.

Madeira
a type of wine.

Madras
1) cotton or rayon shirt material; 2) a large silk or cotton kerchief.

Maeser
a wooden drinking bowl.

Maize
a type of Indian corn.

Malaga
a type of white wine.

Mall
var. of maul.

Mallet
a hammer-like tool made of wood.

Mammy bench
a small settee with rockers and a removable gate that was used as a cradle.

Manchet
the finest kind of wheat bread.

Mandilion
a loose, full frock, falling straight to about mid-thigh with hanging sleeves.

Mangle
a machine for smoothing cloth, originally between a reciprocating weighted box or plate and a lower polished plate; later between two rollers.

Mangle bat
a flat piece of wood used in conjunction with a wooden roller to wring clothes: clothes were wrapped around the roller and the mangle bat rolled against it.

Manta
1) a blanket or cloth for a horse or mule; 2) a kind of cloak or wrap; 3) ordinary cotton cloth; 4) a cover for a pack on a pack-saddle.

Manteau
1) a mantua; 2) a loose robe, negligee, or mantle.

Mantua
1) a type of fabric, probably silk; 2) a lady's gown without straps; a loose-bodied robe, usually an overdress resembling

a mantle, worn with an underdress or with a petticoat and stomacher.

Manure knife
a knife with a long, heavy blade for cutting material from a manure pile into manageable pieces, much as a hay knife was used to cut hay from a stack.

Mare
a female horse.

Marking iron
a branding iron.

Marline
a small line of two strands twisted loosely; used for seizing and as a covering for wire rope.

Marlin(e) spike
a tool used for separating the strands of a rope; used for splicing, etc.

Marquisette
a light cotton fabric very loosely woven.

Marseilles
a stout cotton fabric similar to piqué.

Marten
any of several slender-bodied mammals (e.g. sable), prized for their fur; usually used to mean the pelt of a marten.

Martin
var. of marten.

Martingal(e)
a strap fastened to a horse's girth and to the bit; intended to keep a horse from rearing.

Maselin
var. of maeser.

Maser
var. of maeser.

Mask/masque
a mask was often worn by women to protect their faces from sunlight.

Match coat
a fur or coarse woolen mantle or wrap.

Matchlock
an early musket, fired by bringing a lighted slow-match into contact with the priming powder.

Mattock
a heavy tool for digging and grubbing; similar in appearance to a hoe but usually with a double head.

Maul
a pestle-shaped wooden tool used like a hammer.

Maul rings
metal bands put around maul heads to keep the wood from splitting.

Maulkin
a mop for the hearth of an oven.

Maund
a wicker basket.

Mazer/mazur
vars. of maeser.

Mead
a drink made from fermented honey.

Medder/meader
a wooden cup with handles and feet.

Merino
a breed of sheep.

Met
1) a unit or instrument of measuring, usually a bushel; 2) a unit of measure usually = a bushel; 3) var. of meat.

Metheglin
a beverage of fermented honey and water.

Mether
a wooden goblet.

Metzo-
phonetic spelling of mezzo-.

Mezzotint(o)
a type of engraving made by removing or smoothing parts of the previously roughened surface of a steel or copper plat.

Middling
of medium or intermediate size or quality.

Mill brass
probably a grinding plate for a hand operated mill.

Mill pick
a pick hammer used to dress millstones.

Milled dollar
= piece of eight.

Miquelet lock
a type of flintlock.

Mobcap
a cap or bonnet for women, especially one with a full crown and frills, fastened under the chin.

Mohair
wool from the angora goat or cloth made from such wool.

Moidore
a Portuguese gold coin worth about $3.27.

Moleskin
same as terry velvet but used for clothing.

Money scales
a set of scales designed to be used for weighing precious metals.

Moreen
a coarse, stout cloth of wool or wool and cotton.

Morella
a fabric used for dresses and draperies.

Morello
the color mulberry (reddish-blue of very low saturation and brilliance).

Morgan
a breed of light horses.

Morning dress
1) a woman's dress suitable for wear around the home; 2) formal daytime attire for men consisting of a cutaway coat or frock coat, fancy waistcoat, and gray or black-and-white striped trousers; 3) see also mourning.

Morocco
a type of leather.

Mortar and pestle
a cup-shaped container (mortar) and a club-shaped piece (pestle) used for pulverizing materials.

Mosling
a thin shred of leather shaved off in dressing skins.

Mosquito bar
a rough cotton fabric.

Mouldbaert
a leveling box used to move sail from high to low spots.

Mo(u)ldboard
a part of a plow behind the share which turns over the furrow.

Mourning
referring to a period of bereavement; see also morning dress.

Mourning cloak
a black cloak for wear at funerals.

Mourning jewelry
jewelry, usually rings, pins, or lockets but sometimes earrings or bracelets, given to mourners at a funeral in rembrance of the deceased. They often had pictures or brief biographies of the deceased on them and sometimes contained the hair of the deceased arranged in ingenious patterns.

Mourning presents
various items were presented to mourners or to clergymen at funerals. Jewelry has already been mentioned, but articles of clothing, especially gloves, were sometimes given.

Mov(e)ables
personal property that can be carried from place to place, as opposed to real property.

Muck cart
a cart with high sides used to carry manure to fields.

Muck spreader
a trailer for distributing manure to fields.

Muckle wheel
a wool wheel.

Mulatto
in general usage, any person of mixed Caucasian and Negro blood. The term **Indian mulatto** has also been seen, presumably referring to a person of mixed Caucasian and Indian blood.

Muller
a stone or thick lump of glass or metal used as a pestle for grinding grains, pigments, drugs, etc.

Mummy cloth
a cotton or linen cloth with a rough texture.

Murrey
var. of morello.

Muscovado/musco sugar
unrefined or raw sugar, obtained from sugar cane by evaporating the juice and draining off the molasses.

Muscovy duck
a type of domesticated duck (*Carina moschata*).

Musket
a type of long gun with a smooth bore (i.e. no rifling).

Musketoon
a short form of musket, usually carried by cavalry.

Muslin
a fine cotton cloth of plain weave.

Myrtle wax
= bayberrywax.

Nainsook
a light, white cotton cloth with a glossy finish on one side.

Nankeen
1) a firm-textured cotton cloth, usually yellowish-brown; 2) (plural) trousers made of such cloth.

Napkin
1) same meaning as today; 2) a handkerchief; 3) a kerchief or neckerchief; 4) an infant's diaper.

Naples red
1) a red ochre (q.v.); 2) Indian red (q.v.).

Naples yellow
basic lead antimonate, used as a pigment.

Nappery
table linen.

Narrow-ax(e)
probably refers to any of several types
of axes, including felling axes; "narrow"
seems to be used simply to indicate that
it is not a "broad"-ax.

Narrowboat
a type of canal boat.

Navigraph
a type of sextant.

Neat
cattle or oxen; sometimes used to refer
to leather made from hides of such animals.

Neat's-foot oil
oil made by boiling the feet and shin
bones of neat cattle; used to treat leather.

New blue
ultramarine (synthetic).

Nib
a two-wheeled cart for lifting and drag-
ging logs.

Niddy-noddy
= cross reel.

Night chair
= closestool.

Night lamp
a lamp with a small flame, designed to
burn all night.

Night table
probably = closestool.

Nightgown
a type of men's dressing gown.

Nightstool
= closestool.

Nocturnal
a navigational instrument for determining time at night by stellar observations.

Noggin
1) a wooden pitcher and drinking vessel
made from one piece of wood; cf. tankard; 2) a unit of measure = 1/2 cup.

None-so-pretty
a kind of decorative braid or tape.

North pistol
a pistol made by Simeon North, a gun-
smith who supplied the U. S. Navy.

Nozzle
the socket for a candle on a candlestick
or sconce.

Nun's cloth/nun's thread
a fine woolen bunting used for dresses.

Nuremburg diptych/sundial
a type of portable sundial.

Nutgall
a nut-like swelling of plant tissues caused
by bacteria, viruses, parasites, etc.; they
contain a large amount of tannin and
are used as a commercial source of it.

Oast
a kiln, usually for hops or malt.

Occamy
var. of alchemy.

Ocher/ochre
an earthy ore of iron, usually red or yellow; used as a pigment.

Octant
a type of navigational instrument.

Oil cloth/oil skin
cloth treated with oil or paint to make it
waterproof.

Open cupboard
a cupboard with a doorless top, two or
more shelves, and a lower section that
is closed.

Organdy/organdie
a very thin, stiff cotton fabric.

Orgeat
a syrup made from barley or almonds, or a drink flavored with such syrup.

Oriental lowestoft
any Chinese porcelain made for European markets.

Orpiment
a mineral, As S , used as a yellow pigment.

Osnaburg
a coarse linen fabric.

Ottoman
a fabric made from silk and cotton.

Oven rake
a tool with a hoe-like head, used to clean ashes out of an oven that has been heated.

Oxford
a cotton fabric woven in basket weave.

Oxford down
a breed of sheep.

Oyster knife
a knife with a short, stout blade for opening oysters.

Pace-weight
a loom attachment to keep the warp even.

Pack thread/twine
strong thread or small twine used for sewing or tying packs and parcels.

Packet-ship
one of various types of seagoing vessels, square rigged.

Paddy/padi
unmilled rice, whether cut or still growing.

Paduasoy
a rich, heavy, corded silk fabric.

Paint stone
probably a type of mortar used with a muller for grinding pigments.

Pallet
a small bed.

Palm
a sailmaker's tool for sewing and roping sails.

Panel
1) a saddle pad; 2) a wooden saddle for a donkey.

Pannier
1) a wicker basket for carrying things while on a horse; 2) a hooped outer garment for a woman.

Pantry
a room where food and provisions are stored, usually off the kitchen.

Paragon
1) a cloth like double camblet; used for clothing and upholstery; 2) a kind of black marble.

Parallel ruler
two or more rulers joined by hinged strips; used for laying out courses on a chart.

Paregoric
a camphorated tincture of opium; used as a painkiller.

Parlor
the "company room" of a house; often served as a guest bedroom.

Partisan/partizan
a long-handled, pike-like weapon.

Paste
a lead glass composition of great

brilliance; used to imitate stones such as diamonds.

Patch box
a container, usually of leather, in which cloth or hide patches were carried for use with muzzle-loading rifles or muskets.

Patent medicines
any of a large group of premade medicines, often made and marketed by individuals; some of them were: Anderson's (Scotch) Pills; Lockyer's Pills; British Oil; Bateman's (Pectoral) Drops; Stoughton's Drops; Daffy's Elixir (Salutis); Dutch Drops; Elixir Salutis; Spirit of Scurvy-Grass (golden/plain); Bitter Stomach Worm Drops; Turlington's Balsom (of Life); Hooper's (Female) Pills; Lavender & Hungary Water; Hill's Balsom of Honey; Benton's True & Genuine British Oil; Godfrey's General Cordial; Walker's Jesuit's Drops; Essence of Peppermint; Swinsen's Electuary; Royal Honey Water; Turlington's Remedy for Every Malady; Dalby's Carminative; Stoughton's Elixir.

Pattens
a form of overshoe resembling a raised platform, worn by women to protect their shoes outside the house.

Patty pan
a pan for baking patties (little pies or pastries).

Pavillion
1) a type of tent; 2) a canopy for a bed.

Pea jacket
a thick, loose, woolen, double-breasted coat or jacket.

Peak
a type of lace.

Peat
a vegetable material found in bogs; when dried, used as a fuel for fire.

Peat knives and spades
tools in a variety of shapes for cutting peat.

Peavey
a log-handling tool combining the cant hook and the jam pike.

Peel
a broad, thin board with a long handle; used to put bread into out take it out of an oven.

Peeling
a thin dress material.

Peeling chisel
a tool for removing bark from logs to hasten drying.

Peer glass
a mirror.

Pekoe
a type of tea.

Pelham
a curb bit for horses.

Peliss
a type of cloak.

Pembroke (table)
a small drop-leaf table whose top is essentially square when the leaves are up; the edge of the top may be cut in a serpentine shape.

Pencil post
a posted bed whose posts are long and slender; it sometimes has a canopy.

Penniston
a woolen cloth used for linings.

Percale
a finely woven cotton fabric.

Percent
as in the root meaning of the word, "for each hundred."

Perch
a unit of measure = 1 rod = 1/4 chain = 16 1/2 feet = 1 pole.

Percheron
a breed of draft horses.

Periagua
= piragua.

Perpet(uana)/perpetuo
a type of serge.

Perry
a fermented liquor made from pears; pear cider.

Persian
1) often used indiscriminately to refer to something of Near-Eastern origin; 2) used alone, usually a thin silk fabric.

Persian red
= Indian red.

Peruvian bark
= cinchona.

Petronel
a type of firearm halfway between a pistol and a musket in size.

Petticoat
1) a short undercoat worn by men; 2) a waistcoat; 3) a skirt, especially one showing under an overskirt or dress; 4) an underskirt.

Pewter cupboard
= open cupboard.

Phaeton
a light, four-wheeled carriage with or without a top, having one or two seats.

Phial
a vessel or bottle, especially a small glass bottle for medicines; a vial.

Phil(l)ip & Cheney
a woolen cloth.

Phoebe-lamp
a lamp similar to a Betty-lamp, but larger.

Pickaroon
a tool about the size of an ax but with a beak-like head; used for handling logs.

Pick-ax
a tool for digging; a pick.

Pick-up baler
a machine to gather and bale hay in the field.

Pie safe
a closed cupboard whose door panels are hand-pierced pieces of tin or sometimes wire screening.

Piece
a unit for cloth goods; varies greatly as to size.

Piece of eight
a Spanish silver coin, often over-stamped by other countries; used in the Americas well into the 19th century. See page 28.

Pigeon net
a net used in hunting pigeons; they are driven into it.

Piggin
a small wooden pail with a long stave that serves as a handle.

Pigtail
1) tobacco in small twisted ropes or rolls; 2) a braid of tress (flax that has just been hetcheled).

Pilchard pot
= bussa pot.

Pillion
1) a kind of saddle, as a light one for a

woman, consisting mainly of a cushion; 2) a pad or cushion put on behind a man's saddle for a woman to ride on.

Pillowbere/pillowber/pillowbeer
a pillowcase.

Pillowheer
var. of pillowbeer.

Pilot boat
a trim, fast vessel with schooner rigging.

Pinchbeck
an alloy of copper and zinc; used to imitate gold, usually in cheap jewelry.

Pinchers
usually refers to tongs.

Pink/pinkie/pinky
a sailing vessel with a narrow stern; the name is applied to a variety of types of vessels.

Pinnace
a light sailing vessel, decked and with one or more masts; usually twenty to thirty tons burden.

Pintado
a fine grade of chintz.

Pipe
1) a unit of measure for wine: for Madeira = 110 gallons; for Malaza = 114 gallons; 2) a container of that size.

Pipkin
a small earthenware pot.

Pique
a corded cotton fabric.

Piraqua
a large dugout canoe fitted with sails.

Piroque
a small, open boat with no sails.

Pitchfork
a tined tool used for moving hay.

Pitkin
a type of glass flask, originally made in Connecticut.

Plain
1) plain cloth; 2) sometimes used for plane.

Plane
a tool for surfacing wood. The simplest type (smoothing plane) gives a smooth, flat surface, but there are other types: beading, molding, trying = trueing = long, rabbet, jack, plow, sun.

Plate
a plated object, usually silver. **Plating** is the process by which a thin layer of precious metal is bound to the surface of a more common metal (in early periods, usually silver over copper). Before the mid 1800's the process was chemical; afterwards, electrical.

Plate mill
a mill for grinding meal between metal plates.

Plate warmer
a metal cabinet to keep plates warm until the food is ready to be served.

Plated
1) see plate; 2) see stove.

Pleasure wagon
an open, four-wheeled vehicle with a forward-facing seat mounted on a flat bed; sometimes called a "New England pleasure wagon."

Plow/plough
a tool for tilling soil; types: balance, breast, chisel, disc, foot, subsoil, one-way, paring, reversing, ridging, riding, stump-jump, shovel, swing, turnover, turnwrest, prairie-breaker.

Pocket

not part of a garment as today, but a separate, flat, pear-shaped bag with a vertical slit opening, tied about the waist with a tape.

Pocket book

a book adapted for carrying in a pocket; early records intend this meaning rather than a "purse."

Pod auger

a type of auger with a straight groove, rathen than a spiral channel.

Point

1) any type of lacework; 2) a cord of yarn, silk, or leather used to lace garments.

Poke

a bag or small sack.

Poke-bonnet

a bonnet with a projecting brim.

Poldavis

var. of pouldavines.

Pole

a unit of measure = 16 1/2 feet; same as a rod or perch.

Pomander

1) a perfume or mixture of perfumes enclosed in a bag; 2) a container, often ornate, to hold a perfumed mixture.

Pomatum

a perfumed unguent, especially one for the hair.

Poplin

a fine corded fabric of silk or fine cotton.

Porch

= entry (New England).

Porringer

a dish, bowl, or cup for porridge or similar food.

Port

a fortified wine containing 18-23 percent alcohol; usually dark red, but a white variety exists. Types: vintage port, tawney port, ruby port.

Porter

a mixture of ale and stout.

Portmanteau

an overcoat.

Posnet

a little basin or porringer, sometimes a skillet, and sometimes on a tripod base.

Poss stick

= posser.

Posser

a variation on the dolly stick.

Posset

a beverage of hot milk, curdled by the infusion of ale, wine, etc., and often containing spices.

Post chaise

basically a chariot (q.v.) without the driver's seat.

Potash

K_2CO_3, especially that obtained from leaching wood ashes; used in soap making.

Pot brake

= pot hook.

Pot claw

= pot hook.

Pot clip

= pot hook.

Pot crook

= pot hook.

Pot fork

= flesh fork.

Pot hanger
= pot hook.

Pot hook
a simple, S-shaped hook used to suspend pots from a crane (q.v.), trammel bar (q.v.), etc. A **rachette pot hook** is a pot hook with a handle that allows a kettle to be tipped without removing it from the hook.

Pot metal
1) a cast iron used for making pots and other hollow-ware; 2) an alloy of copper with much lead.

Pottinger
= porringer.

Pottle
1) a liquid or dry measure = 1/2 gallon; 2) a pot or tankard of about 1/2 gallon capacity; 3) a vessel or small basket for holding fruit.

Pouldavines
a coarse canvas.

Powder blue
powdered smalt (q.v.) used for laundering.

Powder box
1) a box for gunpowder; 2) a box for salt or spices; 3) a box for cosmetic powder.

Powder flask
a wood or metal container with a narrow pouring spout for loading black powder into a rifle or musket.

Powder horn
a container similar to a powder flask but made from an animal's horn.

Powdering tub
a tub in which meat is corned or salted.

Ppette
= perpetuana.

Press
1) an upright case or closet for the safe-keeping of articles; 2) a large cupboard.

Press bed
a bed which is set wholly within or folds into a press or cupboard with doors.

Press cupboard
a short, two-part cupboard with a step-back; the upper case is a closed cupboard and the lower is a closed cupboard or drawers.

Pricker
a sailmaker's tool.

Primer
1) originally a prayer book containing the Little Office, Office of the Dead, psalms, prayers, etc., and used to teach children to read; 2) any small elementary book for teaching children to read.

Princess
a type of fabric.

Prismatic compass
a compass with a prism so that the compass card and the object being sighted can be seen simultaneously.

Promes
dried plums or prunes.

Prospective glass
= spyglass.

Protractor
an instrument with graduated scales used for determining angles.

Prunella
a type of black-dyed shalloon cloth.

Prussian blue
any of several cyanogen compounds of

iron; used as pigments in paint, dyes, inks, and as bluing for the laundry.

Psalter
a psalm book.

Pump
1) a device for moving liquids; 2) a low shoe, gripping the foot only at the heel and toe.

Puncheon
1) a large cask; 2) a split log.

Pung
a small sled with a box attached.

Punt
a small, flat-bottomed boat, usually with a seat in the middle and a well or seat at one end; rowed or poled in shallow waters.

Purslin
a type of china originally from India.

Pyramid
a set of pedestal-based salvers of decreasing size to be stacked on a table for displaying foods.

Quadrant
a navigational instrument similar to a sextant.

Quaich/Quaigh
a wooden-staved cup with two ears; later, a two-eared cup of any material.

Quarn
var. of quern.

Quarrel
var. of quarry.

Quarry
1) a pane of glass; 2) a tile.

Quarter
a unit of weight for cereals = about 8 bushels.

Quebec
perhaps a type of lace.

Queen's-arm
a colloquial term for a musket.

Queen's-ware
a glazed English earthenware of a cream color.

Quern
a simple, hand-operated mill for grains.

Quill
a bobbin used in weaving to hold thread for the weft.

Quill winder
= quilling wheel.

Quilling wheel
a device for wrapping thread or yarn on bobbins (quills or spools).

Quilt
1) originally a kind of mattress, now a bed coverlet; 2) a quilted underskirt.

Quilting
any cloth that has a pattern-like quilted work.

Quilting frame
a frame-like device on which a quilt is held while being sewn.

Quire
1) a group of twenty-four or twenty-five pieces of paper; 2) a small book or pamphlet; 3) a work: poem, essay, etc.

Quoddy boat
a partially decked fishing boat, the hull tapering at both ends and usually having one mast.

Rabbet saw
a tool that looks like a plane, but has a saw along one edge rather than a blade; used for making rabbets.

Rachette pot hook
see pot hook.

Raddle
a loom attachment, consisting of a wooden bar with a row of closely set, fine wooden pegs; used in setting the warp threads to insure proper width.

Raft shackles
two metal spikes linked with a chain; used for fastening logs together into rafts.

Raival
= raddle.

Rake
= raddle.

Ram
a male sheep.

Range
a kitchen grate.

Rapier
a sword with a long, straight, slender blade.

Rash
a type of silk or silk and wool cloth.

Rasp
a device similar to a file but with coarser teeth; used for shaping wood.

Ratline(e)
a small, usually three-stranded, tarred rope used in ship rigging.

Ratteen
a general term used of heavy woolen cloths.

Rave hook
a tool used in caulking boats.

Ravel
= raddle.

Real property
land or that which is attached to the land (e.g. buildings) as opposed to chattels.

Ream
a quantity of paper, the number of sheets within which varies with the type of paper, but is usually 472-516. See also reamer.

Ream(er)
a tool for enlarging or shaping holes.

Reap(ing) hook
a long, slender sickle.

Rebate
var. of rabbet.

Recon
a pot hook.

Recorder
a wooden musical instrument; the precursor of the transverse flute.

Red lead
Pb_3O_4, powdered and used as a paint pigment.

Red polled
a breed of dairy cattle.

Redware
a type of stoneware.

Redwood
the powdered wood of any of several trees; when properly treated, it yields an intense red dye.

Reed
= sley.

Reed-hook
= sley-hook.

Reel
a revolvable device on which yarn or thread is wound into hanks or skeins.

Refine
sometimes used for "refined," which can have different meanings, depending on the context; more usual meanings include "clarified" as with wine, and "polished" as with metals.

Reflecting circle
an instrument used for measuring horizontal and vertical angles; used for navigation and surveying.

Rep(p)/reps
a corded upholstery fabric of wool, silk, or cotton or a combination of them.

Reticule
a net bag or purse.

Rhenish stoneware
a type of pottery, often with a mottled brown pattern, but also in gray.

Rhumboscope
an instrument used to locate positions on a chart.

Rhysimeter
an instrument for determining a ship's speed.

Riddle
a sieve with a coarse mesh.

Riding chair
a two-wheeled, single passenger vehicle, consisting of a chair mounted on a framework.

Riff
= straik.

Rifle
a type of long gun, into the barrel of which grooves (rifling) are cut. They make the bullet spin, giving it increased range and accuracy. Types: Pennsylvania, Kentucky, later brandnames such as Winchester.

Ring bolt
an eyebolt with a ring through it.

Ring dial
= Gemma's ring.

Ripe stick
= straik.

Ripple comb
a device for removing seeds from flax fibers.

Roan
1) a muted yellow-red color, often applied to animals; 2) phonetic spelling of Rouen.

Rockaway
1) a low, light, four-wheeled carriage with a standing top, open at the sides but with waterproof curtains; 2) a similar but heavier carriage, enclosed except in the front and having a door on each side.

Rocking settee
= nanny bench.

Rod
a unit of measure = 16 1/2 feet.

Rojas dial
a type of portable sundial.

Roller crusher
a machine for bruising cut grass.

Romal
var. of rumal.

Romney
a breed of sheep.

Rood
1) a unit of measure, varied locally but usually 5 1/2-8 yards; 2) a unit measure = 1/4 acre.

Roquelaure
a type of cloak.

Roqueloe
probably a var. of roquelaure.

Roster
var. of roaster.

Rouen
1) faïence; 2) a breed of domestic duck.

Rough rice
= paddy.

Round
sometimes used for rung (as in a ladder).

Roundabout chair
 = corner chair.

Royal Honey Water
a patent medicine (q.v.).

Rubstone
a whetstone or a grit for scouring or polishing.

Ruddle
red ochre; used as a pigment.

Ruffler
a coarse hetchel.

Rug
any bed or table cover; cf. carpet.

Rule
a ruler.

Rumal
a fabric of cotton or silk from India.

Rummer
a drinking glass with a disproportionately large bowl.

Rump
a pad stuffed with cork, fitted to the back of the waist and tied with tapes in the front.

Rundlet
1) a small barrel; 2) a canteen.

Runge
an oval tub with handles.

Runlet
var. of rundlet.

Rush-bottomed
usually applied to chairs: having a seat made of interwoven rushes, the leaves of the plants *Juncus* sp. or *Scirpus* sp.

Russel
a woolen cloth used for clothing.

Russel cord
a wool and cotton cloth used for women's dresses, bags, etc.

Russet
1) a homespun cloth of coarse texture; 2) a reddish-brown color; 3) sometimes to indicate something coarse or rustic, regardless of its color.

Russia leather
leather made from various skins by tanning with barks of willow, birch, or oak and then rubbing the flesh side with birch oil.

Rutter
a book containing information on tides, sailing directions, maritime routes, etc.

Saber/sabre
a sword with a broad, slightly curved blade about thirty inches long.

Sack
any of various strong white wines from southern Europe; originally (before 1600) applied to any dry wine.

Sack hook
a handled hook for lifting sacks.

Sackcloth
a coarse fabric of flax or hemp.

Sad ware
a generic term for cast iron utensils without a hollow interior (e.g. plates); cf. hollow-ware.

Sadiron
a flatiron for smoothing cloth.

Safeguard
a long over-petticoat to protect the gown from mud and rain, especially when riding a horse.

Sagathy
cloth: a type of serge.

Sago
a dry, granulated or powdered starch used in cooking or in stiffening textiles.

Salamander
a browning iron with a long handle; used to brown or toast the surface of roasts or pastry.

Saler
= saltcellar.

Salt
a container for salt at the table; a saltcellar.

Saltcellar
a vessel, made of various materials, used on the table for holding salt.

Saltpeter/saltpetre
any of several nitrate salts (K_2NO_3, Na_2NO_3, $CaNO_3$) used in making gunpowder and medicinally.

Salvatory
a box or receptacle for ointment.

Salver
a drip-pan.

Sand glass
a time measuring device, now generally called an hour glass.

Sandarac/gum sandarac
a faintly aromatic, translucent resin of the sandarac tree; used in making varnish and as an incense.

Sars(e)nett(e)
a fine silk cloth used for linings.

Sash
as a woman's outer garment, = girdle, definition #2.

Sash glass
= window glass.

Satin
a heavy silk fabric.

Satinet/sateen/satine
an imitation satin fabric made with yarns other than silk.

Sausage funnel
a funnel used to stuff ground meat into sausage casings.

Sausage gun
a cylinder with a funnel-like tip into which ground meat is placed, followed by a piston, so that it can be forced into casings.

Saw set
a tool used to offset the teeth of a saw to a fixed angle with respect to the plane of the blade.

Saw-buck
a device for holding wood while it is sawed.

Saw-buck table
rectangular table whose legs are x-shaped and connected by a long stretcher.

Saxon(y) wheel
a type of flax wheel.

Say
a fabric, a type of serge.

Scarne
in weaving, a rack to hold spools when measuring off warp threads.

Schoolmaster's desk
essentially a desk box with legs; there may be drawers below the box.

Schooner
a sailing vessel with two or more masts, rigged with at least two fore-and-aft sails and a jib.

Schrank
= kas.

Sconce
1) a candlestick or group of candlesticks, often with a mirror to reflect the light; designed to be placed against a wall; 2) a flat candlestick with a handle; 3) a screened lantern or candlestick.

Scorp
an edged tool used for hollowing wood (e.g. for bowls, troughs, etc.).

Scotch hands
wooden paddles, ribbed on one side, for working butter.

Scow
a large, flat-bottomed boat with square ends and straight sides.

Scratter
= grapple.

Scripto(i)r(e)
probably a secretary desk.

Scruitore
var. of scriptoire.

Scutcheon
var. of escutcheon.

Scutching block and knife
= swingling block and knife.

Scuttle
a wide, shallow basket or pail.

Scythe
a two-handed tool used for cutting grasses.

Seal
any device bearing a design, intended for making an impression on wax or clay.

Searce(r)/searse(r)
a fine sieve.

Search(er)
var. of searce.

Secretary (desk)
a two-part piece of furniture: the lower part is similar to a slant-top desk and the upper is a bookcase or cupboard.

Sector
a mathematical measuring instrument, basically a jointed ruler; used for making geometrical and trigonometrical calculations in navigation and gunnery.

Seed drill
a device for planting seeds in rows.

Seed fiddle
a carried mechanical device for broadcast sowing of seed.

Seed-lac
see lac.

Seersucker
a linen or silk fabric with repeated rippled stripes running lengthwise.

Sempitername
a durable woolen cloth.

Serge
a twilled, worsted fabric, often of silk or fine linen.

Servant
see indenture.

Set
1) a group of related objects; 2) used to qualify any of several types of tools, as "set hammer"; 3) sometimes misused to mean suit.

Setbolt
an iron pin or bolt for setting planks closely together, usually in shipbuilding.

Settee
a bench seat with a back and arms; it looks most like a very wide chair.

Setter
1) a jack (for carriages); 2) a low, short sawhorse on which a carriage axle is placed to keep the wheel off the ground.

Settle bed
a bench-like piece of furniture so constructed that it can be converted into a sleeping box.

Settle table
= hutch table.

Sextant
a navigational instrument for determining latitude and longitude.

Sgraffito/sgraffiato
pottery or ware decorated by scratching through a surface layer of glazing, revealing a different colored ground.

Shagreen
a type of leather with a pebbled surface; dyed various bright colors, but often green.

Shakefork
a type of pitchfork, usually made of wood.

Shalloon
a cloth of 100 percent worsted wool.

Shallop
a small boat, open or half-decked, with one or two masts for use if needed; used for fishing, oystering, hauling trade goods, etc.

Shamble
1) a stool or footstool; 2) a counter, bench, or table for market merchandise, especially meat.

Share
the pointed cutter of a plow.

Sharpie
a long, sharp, flat-bottomed boat with one or two masts, fore-and-aft rigged.

Sheffield(ware)
any object silver plated in the manner of Sheffield, England.

Sherry-vallies
an overgarment to protect the trousers from mud and rain, especially when riding a horse.

Shift
a woman's garment.

Ship
technically, a sailing vessel with three or more masts, square rigged; often used for any type of vessel.

Shire
a breed of heavy draft horses of great size.

Shoat
a young hog.

Shorthorn
a breed of dairy cattle or beef cattle.

Shot
spheres of lead for use as ammunition; various qualifiers are usually added, which in general indicate the size: (largest to smallest) grape, buck, goose, bird.

Shropshire
a breed of sheep.

Shuttle
a device for placing weft threads between warp threads in weaving; types: boat, throw, rug.

Sickle
a tool like a curved knife for cutting grasses.

Sideboard
a rectangular table with drawers below the top; used in dining rooms as a place from which to serve food.

Sillabub
a dish made by mixing wine or cider with milk, forming a soft curd; also sweetened cream, flavored with wine and beaten to a stiff froth.

Singletrees
= whippletrees.

Sith hook
an early type of scythe.

Sitting room
usually = parlor.

Skarne
= scarne.

Skein
a measure of thread or yarn, usually consisting of forty loops, but the number varied.

Skep
a beehive made of straw ropes bound together in a spiral fashion.

Skewer
a pointed rod of metal or wood; used to fasten meat to be roasted to a spit.

Skiff
a light, swift, open boat, double-ended for rowing, but sometimes rigged for sailing.

Skim coulter
a small cutter to turn over the top of the slice ahead of a plowshare.

Slant-lip/top desk
essentially a chest of drawers with a lid slanting at a 45-degree angle; the lid folds down to form a writing surface and the exposed inside of the top reveals small drawers and/or pigeon-holes.

Slasher
a long-handled billhook.

Sleeker
any of various flat, cylindrical or wedge-shaped tools used in working hides.

Sleek-stone
a stone used in burnishing; probably sometimes intended to mean a sharpening stone.

Sley
a part of a loom, consisting of a row of short, very thin, parallel strips of cane or metal which, when inserted in the batten, is used to force newly placed weft threads into place.

Sley-hook
a tool for placing warp threads between the dents (slots) of a sley.

Slice
a peel or spatula.

Slick
a large framing chisel.

Slipper chair
a chair with a purposely low seat

Slipping
= skein.

Slipware
pottery coated with slip (a liquified potter's clay) to improve the surface or change the color.

Sloop
a sailing vessel with a single mast, fore-and-aft rigged, often only a mainsail and jib.

Slop basin
1) a basin or bowl for receiving the rinsings of tea or coffee cups at the table; 2) a basin or bowl for waste water from cleaning.

Small beer
a weak beer.

Small clothes
1) close-fitting knee breeches; 2) sometimes, underclothes or children's clothes.

Small sword
a type of hunting sword, much worn by naval officers in the 18th century.

Smalt
a deep blue pigment made by fusing silica potash and cobalt oxide and grinding to a powder.

Smock mill
a mill of mostly wood construction, on which only the cap turns.

Smoke-jack
a device similar to a clock-jack but moved by the current of hot air in the chimney.

Smoothbore
a musket.

Smuggler's keg
a small cask, holding about 3 1/2 pints.

Snaffle
a type of horse bit.

Snakeroot
the root of various plants, but especially *Aristolochia serpentaria*; used as a medicinal herb.

Snaphaan/snaphaunce
a flintlock.

Snaplock
a type of flintlock.

Snath
= snead.

Snead
the handle for a scythe.

Sneak cup
a small cup.

Snitzel-knife
Pennsylvania German word for draw-knife.

Snow
a seagoing vessel with two masts rigged like a brig but with an additional mast rigged with a goff-headed trysail.

Snuffer
a device for trimming candle wicks.

Soder
old spelling and phonetic of solder.

Solder
(pronounced sod´ er) an alloy of lead and tin used in soldering metals.

Solitaire
1) a single gemstone (usually a diamond) set alone; hence a piece of jewelry with a single stone; 2) a large silk neckcloth worn by men.

Sorg(h)um/sorgo
a cane crop grown for forage and for its syrup.

Sorrel
1) a plant having a sour juice; used for flavoring; 2) a brown, red-yellow color; 3) a horse of sorrel color.

Southdown
a breed of sheep.

Sow
a female hog.

Spangle
a small plate or boss of shining metal used as an ornament; often stitched to a dress.

Spanish brown
a dark red-brown pigment containing iron oxide.

Spanish white
a type of white pigment; bismuth subnitrate.

Spatter-dashes
= sherry-vallies.

Spermaco(e)ti
a white waxy material from whales used for making candles (of very high quality), ointments, etc.

Spider
1) a frying pan with legs and a long handle for use in fireplaces; 2) a trivit; 3) a tripod.

Spike hoe
= grapple.

Spinel
bleached yarn used to make inkles.

Spinet
a small form of harpsichord.

Spinnel
var. of spindle.

Spirit of Scurvy-Grass (golden/plain)
a patent medicine (q.v.).

Spit
a metal device, often only a pointed rod, for roasting meat; they later became more intricate and often specialized.

Spittle
1) a kind of spade-like implement; 2) a peel.

Spoke shave
an edged tool similar to a draw-knife but with a shorter, sometimes curved blade; used for making round spokes for wheels.

Spool
a bobbin used in weaving to hold thread for the warp.

Spool-holder
a device for holding an assemblage of spools in weaving.

Spotted chambray
a yarn-dyed cotton cloth woven in two colors.

Spreader
1) a device to hold two singletrees apart; a doubletree; 2) an implement for spreading manure; 3) a gambrel; 4) a temple for a loom.

Spyglass
a hand-held telescope.

Square
an instrument with at least one right angle and two or more straight edges; used to lay out or test square work; many are combination tools capable of determining many angles.

Staffordshire
a type of china.

Staffs
dialectic var. of Staffordshire.

Stag
1) can refer to the male of many species, especially deer; 2) a male animal, castrated after the secondary sex characteristics have developed.

Stake
= handiron, definition #1.

Stale
a handle for a tool, especially a rake or fork.

Stallion
a male horse.

Stammel
a coarse woolen fabric, usually dyed red.

Stanchion
a device which fits loosely around an animal's neck and limits forward and backward movement while permitting a lateral swinging motion.

Stanner
= stenner.

Stannery/stennery
items made of tin.

Stay
1) (usually plural) a corset stiffened with whalebone or other material; the singular form is used in combined forms like stay-lace; 2) a fastening for a garment; a clasp; a hook.

Stean/steen
a vessel or receptacle of clay or stone.

Steel
1) virtually anything customarily made of steel, as knives and swords; 2) an instrument for sharpening knives; 3) an instrument for striking sparks from a flint.

Steel pencil
probably a scratch awl, used for making marks on softer metals like brass.

Steelyard
a type of scale with a moveable weight and calibrated arm.

Steer
a male bovine animal castrated before sexual maturity; cf. stag.

Stenner/Stanner
a measuring scoop for grains, etc., usually made of tin, but sometimes of wood.

Stennery
var. of stannery.

Step-back cupboard
a two-part cupboard, the upper section of which is not so deep as the lower, leaving a shelf exposed at the top of the lower section.

Stickle
= riff.

Stiletto
1) a long, thin-bladed knife; 2) a bodkin.

Stillage
a stool, bench, stand, etc., to keep something from touching the floor, as a support for a tapped cask or in a bleachery to hold up textiles and yarns while they drain.

Stil(l)gart
a dialectic var. of steelyard.

Stilling
a stillion.

Stillion
a stand, as for vats in a brewery.

Stillyard
var. of steelyard.

Stock buckle
a buckle to secure a cravat.

Stock lock
a lock enclosed in a wooden case and attached to the face of a door.

Stomacher
1) an ornamental covering for the front of the upper body, worn by both men and women; 2) a brooch or plaque, worn at chest level.

Stone
1) a generic term for any precious or semi-precious stone; 2) a unit of weight, usually = fourteen pounds.

Stone blue
ground azurite; used as a blue pigment.

Stone yellow
a yellow ochre.

Stoneboat
a flat, runnerless sled used for hauling heavy material; used in summer as well as winter.

Stoneware
generally, any heavy ceramic container.

Stoughton's Drops
a patent medicine (q.v.).

Stoughton's Elixir
a patent medicine (q.v.).

Stout
a malt liquor brewed with malt and toasted malt.

Stove
Wood-burning stoves are often described as being "x-plated" (where x = a number). This is the number of cooking holes, each covered by a plate when not in use, and it gives an idea of the size of the stove.

Stradsticks
= whippletrees.

Straik(e)
an instrument used for sharpening scythes; it was a grooved wooden paddle with a grease and sand mixture held by the grooves.

Straw knife
= hay knife.

Streaked calico
a calico cloth with narrow blue and white stripes.

Strickle
= straik.

Striped stuff
a generic term for cotton and/or woolen fabric.

Strong waters
distilled spirits.

Strop
a leather strap for sharpening a razor.

Stuff
wool cloth, plain or twilled.

Suffolk
1) a breed of draft horses; 2) either of two breeds of hogs.

Sugar box/pot
a sugar bowl.

Sugar cutters/shears
a device for cutting loaf sugar or cone sugar into lumps.

Sugar hatchet
a hatchet-like tool for breaking up sugar loaves.

Sugar loaf
1) a loaf or mass of refined sugar, weighing usually nine to ten pounds; the form in which sugar was purchased; 2) a type of hat shaped like a sugar loaf.

Sugar shears
= sugar cutters.

Suit
sometimes used in the sense of "set," as in a "suit of curtains."

Sulky
a vehicle similar to a chaise but for one person.

Summer cloth
canvas or waterproofed sailcloth.

Surrey
a four-wheeled pleasure carriage with two forward-facing seats and sometimes with a top.

Surtout
a man's overcoat, usually long and close-fitting.

Susi
a striped fabric of cotton and silk.

Swage
a blacksmith's tool for bending metal.

Swanskin
closely woven flannel.

Sweet oil
any mild, edible oil, such as olive oil; often used in medicines.

Sweetmeat
specifically, candied fruit, but often any food rich in sugar, as cake, candy, etc.

Swift
a device for holding yarn or thread being transferred to quills or spools for weaving; types: cross-frame, basket, squirrel-cage, umbrella.

Swigler
a small rum keg.

Swine
hogs (usually refers to a group of hogs).

Swing-leg table
a drop-leaf table with two legs that can swing out to support the leaves.

Swingletrees
= whippletrees.

Swingling block and knife
devices used in processing flax: flax was stretched over the block and struck with the knife to remove residual particles of bark.

Swinsen's Electuary
a patent medicine (q.v.).

Swiss
a light, stiff, transparent cotton fabric with a simple embroidered or woven design.

Sword knot
an ornamental ribbon or tassel tied to the hilt of a sword.

Tabine
var. of tobine.

Tackle
1) the accoutrements of work or pastime; 2) an assemblage of ropes and pulleys used to hoist or pull something; 3) the rigging of a ship.

Tackling
1) gear, equipment; 2) the rigging of a ship; 3) harness of a draft animal.

Taffeta/taffety
a fine, smooth, glossy silk or linen fabric.

Tall chest
a chest of drawers with six or more tiers of drawers.

Tallow
hardened animal fat used in making candles and soap.

Tamarind
a tropical tree, the leaves, flowers, and fruit of which are used in dyeing (as a mordant), in preserves, and medicinally; the word is most often used in tanning.

Tambour desk
a desk with a built-in cabinet at the back of the top, the doors of which are thin strips of wood glued to a fabric backing.

Tamellette/tamette/tamad/tamas(e)
a fine worsted cloth, often with a glazed finish.

Tammy
a generic term for any of a group of combed woolen fabrics.

Tankard
a wooden drinking vessel of stave construction, usually with a lid.

Tannin
an amorphous, strongly astringent substance, also called **tannic acid**; used in tanning, dyeing, and inkmaking; also used medicinally as an astringent.

Tap
a hollow tapered cylinder of wood with a valve; driven into the bung hole of a barrel, it is used like a spigot.

Tape loom
a small loom for weaving tapes.

Taper
a small wax candle; later, a long waxed wick.

Tapping gauge
a tool used in setting spouts in maple trees to collect sap.

Tar
usually refers to pine tar.

Tarboggin
= chebobbin.

Tarlatan
a light, sheer, stiff cotton fabric.

Tartan
a woolen cloth with stripes at right angles to each other, forming a pattern (plaid); each Scottish clan had its own pattern.

Taster
see wine taster.

Tavern table
generally, a fairly small, simple, rectangular table, which may have up to two drawers below the top.

Tawed
applied to animal skins, tanned using alum.

Tawny
a yellowish-brown color.

Tea table
any of small, four-legged tables with rectangular or round tops.

Teasel
1) the dried flower head of *Dipsacus fullonum*; used to raise the nap on woolen cloth. A group of them are held in a frame; 2) any contrivance used as a substitute for 1).

Tebobbin
= chebobbin.

Tedder
a machine for tossing and spreading hay to encourage drying.

Temple
a loom attachment made of flat, narrow strips of wood (as long as the web of the cloth is wide) with little hooks or pins at the ends to keep the cloth stretched firmly at an even width.

Tems(e)
a sifter or strainer; a sieve.

Teneriffe
a type of canary wine.

Terraumbra
= umber.

Terrier
a tool for boring holes in wood.

Terry (velvet)
a pile weave cloth with uncut nap.

Test(e) me
(Latin) "witnessed by (me)."

Tester
a fabric canopy for a bed.

Tester bed
a bed with a framework to support a fabric canopy.

Theodolite
a surveying instrument which was an improvement over the circumferentor and graphometer.

Thib(b)le
a skimmer; a spatula.

Thicksett
= corduroy.

Thistle paddle
a framework for holding teasles (q.v.).

Thoroughbrace
leather straps fastened to springs to support a carriage body.

Threaded druggett
a type of linsey-woolsey with corded weave such that the wool is on one side and the linen on the other.

Throw hook
= hay bond twister.

Thunder-and-lightning
a woolen serge.

Ticking
a cotton or linen fabric originally for use in bedding, but also used for heavy-duty clothing.

Ticklengburg
a coarse linen cloth.

Tiffany
a thin, transparent silk or muslin gauze.

Tig
var. of tyg.

Tigerware
Rhenish stoneware.

Tile
usually refers to a decorative ceramic tile, frequently used as a facing for the wall surrounding a fireplace. It was more common in Dutch areas but not rare elsewhere.

Timothy
a grass (*Phleum pratense*) grown as hay.

Timwhiskey
a high, light carriage drawn by one or two horses.

Tinder box
a box containing flint, steel, and tinder for starting fires.

Tinder wheel/mill
a device for starting a fire with flint and steel in which the steel is round and mounted on an axle so it can be spun against a flint.

Tippet
a scarf or scarf-like garment, usually having hanging ends.

Tire
the metal band around the circumference of a wooden wheel; it increases the durability and holds the wooden parts together.

Tissue
a cloth woven of gold or silver thread and silk thread.

Titch crook
a tool with tines set at a right angle to the handle; used to lift dried peat.

Toaster
a metal device for holding bread for toasting by an open fire.

Tobacco boat
a double dugout canoe, fifty to sixty feet long, clamped together with crossbeams and pins, with two pieces running lengthwise over the beams; used to transport hogsheads of tobacco on rivers.

Tobacco knife
a flat-bladed knife with a curved end; used to harvest tobacco.

Tobine
a coarse silk fabric.

Toilet
1) used alone, a cloth used to cover the shoulders while shaving or hairdressing or to cover a dressing table; 2) used in combined forms to describe an article associated with dressing or grooming.

Tombac
an alloy of copper and zinc; used for cheap jewelry, gilding, etc.

Tomble
var. of temple.

Tomyhawk
a twibil or twivel.

Ton/tun
a unit of measure varying from 200 to 2,400 pounds.

Tongs
any of various instruments consisting of two legs hinged together; designed for holding or carrying something.

Tonneken
probably from the Dutch *ton* (barrel), hence a small barrel.

Toss
a drinking cup.

Tow cloth/toe linen
linen cloth which contains fifty percent tow (shorter fibers from flax); poorer quality cloth than Dowlas.

Tower mill
a windmill built of brick or stone on which only the cap turns.

Trace
a piece of harness extending from a collar or yoke to the load being pulled.

Trade cloth
cloth intended for use in trade, especially with Indians; it tended to be coarse and was almost always dyed a bright color.

Trammel
an adjustable pot hook for use in fireplaces.

Trammel bar
a horizontal bar in a fireplace from which pots may be suspended on trammels.

Treble
three times; three-fold.

Treenware
articles made from trees.

Tregar
a linen fabric.

Trencher
a wooden plate.

Trestle
a three-legged stool or bench; but cf. trestle table and bench.

Trestle bench
a bench constructed like a trestle table (q.v.).

Trestle table/board
a table having two pillar-like legs, shaped somewhat like inverted *T*s.

Trivet
a three-legged stand or support of metal to hold a kettle or similar vessel over or near a fire.

Trivet kettle
a kettle with three legs built into its base.

Troll(e)y
1) a type of lace; 2) a type of cart.

Trug
a wooden bucket.

Trumpery
literally, something **deceptively** showy and of no real value; seems to be used as

meaning a bunch of small things of no particular value, much as we would now say, "some junk."

Trundle bed
a very low bed that can be pushed under another bed for storage.

Tumble
var. of temple.

Tumbril
a cart.

Tun
var. of ton.

Tureen
a large deep vessel from which soup is served at the table.

Turkey carpet
an oriental rug.

Turkey leather
a kind of oil-tanned leather.

Turkey umber
see umber.

Turlington's Balsom (of Life)
a patent medicine (q.v.).

Turlington's Remedy for Every Malady
a patent medicine (q.v.).

Turn-furrow
= mouldboard.

Turning chisel
a wood chisel, usually with a long handle; used to cut wood on a lathe.

Turn-up bedstead
a bedstead with the head end hinged to a wall (usually in the kitchen) so that the bed could be swung down at night and up against the wall during the day.

Tutor
a manual of instructions; a textbook.

Tweed
a heavy woolen fabric made from coarse yarn.

Twibil
a T-shaped tool with two chisel heads; used for cutting mortises.

Twiffler
a pudding dish.

Twigged
made of rushes (see rush-bottomed) or wicker.

Twilt
var. of quilt.

Twist
1) a closely twisted, strong sewing silk; 2) a kind of tightly twisted cotton yarn; 3) tobacco in the form of a thick, twisted roll; 4) a material for gun barrels, consisting of iron and steel twisted and welded together.

Twivel
a T-shaped tool similar to a twibil but with the bottom edges of the "T" sharpened rather than the ends; used in making mortises.

Tyg
a kind of drinking cup with two or more handles.

Tyke(n)/tyking
dialectic var. of ticking.

Ultramarine
originally a blue pigment of powdered lapis lazuli, but later made synthetically; used in paints, textiles, printing, papermaking, bluing, etc. The synthetic form came in colors other than blue: yellow and silver.

Umber
a brown earth used as a pigment; **burnt umber** is slightly reddish; the best variety comes from Cyprus and is called **Turkey umber**.

Umbrello/umbrillo
var. of umbrella.

Under-eaves bed
a bedstead with short posts and a low headboard.

Valance
a short decorative drapery that hangs across the top of a window or around the top of a bed.

Valise
a small traveling bag, usually of leather.

Varinas
a type of tobacco from Venezuela.

Vellum
1) a fine-grained lamb, kid, or calf skin; 2) (usually as vellum cloth) a fine cotton fabric, made very transparent; used as a tracing cloth.

Velour
a pile fabric, usually cotton.

Veloutine
corded wool dress fabric with a velvet finish.

Velvet
a short-pile fabric of silk or silk and cotton.

Vendue
auction.

Venetian
1) a heavy kind of tape or braid; 2) a robe for masquerade; 3) a twilled woolen cloth; 4) a twilled and mercerized cotton fabric.

Venetian red
a variety of earth containing ferric oxide; used as a pigment.

Verdigris
a copper compound used as a blue or green (depending on the exact composition) dye and as an external medication (powder or ointment) for skin eruptions.

Verditer
a pigment from either of two basic carbonates of copper: **blue verditer** was originally powdered azurite; **green verditer** was powdered malachite; both are also produced synthetically.

Verge
a unit of length = one yard.

Vermil(l)ion
1) a cotton cloth dyed scarlet; 2) a bright red pigment, originally ground cinnabar.

Vertical compass
= azimuth compass.

Victual(l)er
a tavernkeeper or innkeeper; a grocer.

Vidonia
a type of canary wine.

Virginal
a small rectangular spinet (q.v.) without legs.

Virginia cloth
homespun stuff, usually for use in slaves' clothing.

Virginia plain
= Virginia cloth.

Vitriol
a sulphate of various metals; used in dyes, in varnishes, or medicinally. Types: copper = **blue or Roman vitriol**; iron = **green vitriol**; zinc = **white vitriol**.

Voider
a deep wicker, wooden, or metal basket, into which trenchers, napkins, crumbs, etc., were placed to clear a table.

Voile
a sheer, light fabric.

Wadmoll/wadmell
a coarse woolen fabric.

Wafer iron
two hinged, small griddles, attached to a long handle for baking wafers over a fire.

Wagon seat
a single piece of furniture that looks like two chairs side-by-side; it has only two arms.

Wain
a wagon.

Wainscot
1) applied to a chair, a heavy oak chair with solid panels in the back and seat, often with turned posts and a curved back; 2) applied to other furniture, of heavy oak construction.

Waistcoat
(usually pronounced wes´kit) 1) a man's garment of ornamental character, worn under a doublet; 2) a vest; 3) an undergarment for children, worn around the midriff, to which other garments can be fastened.

Waiter
a vessel or tray on which something is carried; a serving tray.

Walker's Jesuit's Drops
a patent medicine (q.v.).

Walking wheel
a spinning wheel with a very large drive wheel (six or seven feet in diameter); the operator must stand to use it.

Wallet
a bag or sack for carrying personal posses-sions, as on a journey, or for tools or money.

Warming pan
a bed warmer.

Warp-beam
a part of a loom used to hold warp threads.

Warping bar
a loom accessory for measuring simul-taneously a group of warp threads.

Warping frame
= warping bar.

Warping paddle
a wooden paddle with holes at regular intervals; used to guide warp threads during the warping of a loom.

Water bench
= bucket bench.

Wayne
var. of wey.

Weather-skirt
= safeguard.

Wedge
a wedge-shaped piece of wood (a **glut**) or metal used for splitting wood or for exerting side-to-side pressure in joints.

Weeper
a badge of mourning, as 1) a white band or border worn on the cuff; 2) a long black hatband worn by men; 3) (usually plural) the black veil of a widow.

Weigh
var. of wey.

Weir
a fence of stakes, etc., set in a stream or tideway for catching fish.

Welsh dresser
a type of open cupboard.

Wench
can refer to any woman of the peasant class, but in American records always refers to a servant woman and most often a slave.

Weskit
phonetic spelling of waistcoat.

Wether
a ram castrated before the secondary sex characteristics develop.

Wey
a unit of measure for dry goods, varying in size: for cheese, 256-336 pounds; for salt, forty-two bushels.

Whalebone
actually baleen, a horny substance from the upper jaws of baleen whales; often used for stiffening corsets.

Wheel barrow
a wheeled device for moving barrels or other cargo; more similar to today's dolly than to today's wheelbarrow.

Wheel-lock
an early form of flintlock.

Whiffletrees
= whippletrees.

Whippletrees
bars to keep draft chains apart.

Whisk
a woman's neckerchief.

White lead
a white pigment (basic lead carbonate).

White metal
1) any of several lead-base or tin-base metals; 2) any of several white alloys,

such as pewter; 3) a variety of copper with all traces of iron removed.

Whiteware
white pottery in general, often earthenware.

Whiting
chalk (calcium carbonate) used as a pigment and for polishing metals.

Wig block
a round-topped block for making, dressing, or holding a wig.

Wildbore
a woolen fabric for dresses.

Wilton (carpet/rug)
a type of carpet woven with loops which are cut, forming an elastic velvet pile; first made in Wilton, England.

Wimble
1) a tool similar to a gimlet; 2) a kind of brace (tool); 3) an auger to make holes in earth; 4) an instrument for twisting ropes or bonds for tying hay.

Wimple
a covering of silk, linen, or other material, worn by women over the head and around the neck and chin for protection outdoors.

Windsor chair
any chair with spindles and legs socketed into a plank seat; there are numerous types.

Wine taster
a small, shallow silver cup with bosses in the bottom to reflect light and show the color and quality of wine.

Wing
= mouldboard.

Winnowing
the process of separating grain from chaff by means of the wind or a fan; some articles used in the process: winnowing pan, winnowing sieve, winnowing cloth, winnowing fan, winnowing basket.

Wisp
a whisk; a small broom.

Witney
a heavy woolen fabric, napped and shrunk; used in coats and blankets.

Woman saddle
a side-saddle.

Wool comb
a device with long, sharp teeth, similar to a hetchel; used to untangle and soften wool for worsted yarn.

Woolfell
a skin from which the wool has not been sheared or pulled.

Woolwheel
a type of spinning wheel for use with wool.

Woosted
colloquial var. of worsted.

Work table
any table designed primarily as a working surface.

Worm
1) a distilling coil; 2) a corkscrew-shaped tool for removing material from the barrel of a cannon or musket.

Wormed glass
a glass made so that air is tripped in the stem and drawn out into a spiral pattern.

Worsted
1) a smooth-surfaced woolen yarn; 2) any cloth made from such yarn.

Wrap(per)
a loose outer garment similar to a shawl or mantle; "wrapper" actually refers to an indoor garment and "wrap" to an outdoor one, but the differentiation is often ignored.

Wrathe
a raddle.

Writing box
a box with a hinged lid, which serves as a writing surface; a lap desk.

X-cut
an abbreviation: cross-cut.

Yawl
a small sailing vessel rigged like a sloop but with a small additional mast at the stern.

Yearling
an animal in the second year of its life; usually used of horses, cattle, and sheep.

Yell
= evil.

Yellow-ware
= creamware.

Yoke
1) a device to fit the shoulders of humans or animals for carrying or pulling heavy loads; 2) a couple or pair, as in "a yoke of oxen."

Zaag-boc
an early form of sawbuck.

Zephyr
any fine and light fabric.

Abbreviations and Symbols

bbl = barrel

col^d = colored

cwt = hundred weight

- d ("-" is a number) = penny, pence (penny is used to show the size of nails)

dem, di, do = demi = one-half

d^o, do = ditto

fft = fatt

gal, gall = gallon

gl, gll = gill

hhd = hogshead

hk, hks = hank(s)

Imp^s = imprimis

Kln = kilderkin

li = pound

M = 1,000

par, pce, ps = piece

pr, p^2 = pair

qrtr, qtr = quarter

sma = small

To = to wit.

tte = fatt

viz = namely

x = cross

&c, &ca = et cetera

$ = U.S. dollar or Spanish milled dollar

£ = pound (either sterling or local)

Bibliography

Bezanson, Anne, et al., *Wholesale Prices in Philadelphia 1784-1861* (Philadelphia: Univ. of Pennsylvania Press, 1936).

Billings, Warren M., Ed., *The Old Dominion in the Seventeenth Century* (Chapel Hill: Univ. of North Carolina Press, 1975).

Blandford, Percy, *Old Farm Tools and Machinery* (Ft. Lauderdale, Fla.: Gale Research Co., 1976).

Channing, Marion L., *The Textile Tools of Colonial Homes* (Marion, Mass.: Channing Books, 1969, 1971).

Cole, Arthur Harrison, *Wholesale Commodity Prices in the United States 1700-1861, Statistical Supplement* (Cambridge, Mass.: Harvard Univ. Press, 1938).

Dodd, Agnes F., *History of Money in the British Empire and the United States* (London: Longmans, Green & Co., 1911).

Dow, George Francis, *The Arts and Crafts in New England 1704-1775* (Topsfield, Mass.: The Wayside Press, 1927).

Earle, Alice Morse, *Home and Child Life in Colonial Days*, Glubok, Shirley, ed. of revised edition (New York: Macmillan Co., 1969).

_____, *Home Life in Colonial Days* (New York, Grosset & Dunlap, 1968); reprinted by Berkshire Traveller Press, 1974.

Evans, Cerinda W., *Some Notes on Shipbuilding and Shipping in Colonial Virginia* (Richmond, Va.: Garrett & Massie, Inc., 1957).

Gottesman, Rita Susswein, *The Arts and Crafts in New York 1800-1894* (New York, New York Historical Society, 1965).

Gould, Mary Earle, *The Early American House* (New York: Medill McBride Co., 1949).

_____, *Early American Wooden Ware*, revised edition (Springfield, Mass.: Pond-Ekberg Co., 1948).

Hepburn, A. Barton, *A History of Currency in the United States* (New York: The Macmillan Co., 1915).

Hudson, J. Paul, *A Pictorial Booklet on Early Jamestown Commodities and Industries* (Richmond, Va.: Garrett & Massie, Inc., 1957).

Hume, Ivor Noël, *A Guide to Artifacts of Colonial America* (New York: Alfred A. Knopf, Inc., 1969).

_____, *Historical Archaeology* (New York: Alfred A. Knopf, 1980). Note: This book contains an extensive bibliography, broken down by subject matter.

Isham, Norman Morrison, *Early American Houses* (New York: The Walpole Society, DaCapo Press, 1967).

Jones, Alice Hanson, *American Colonial Wealth: Documents and Methods*, 3 vols., 2nd ed. (New York: Arno Press, 1978).

Morris, Richard B., *Government and Labor in Early America* (New York: Octagon Books, 1975).

Morrison, Hugh Sinclair, *Early American Architecture from the First Colonial Settlements to the National Period* (New York: Oxford Univ. Press, 1952).

Nettles, Curtis Putnam, *The Money Supply of the American Colonies before 1720* (Madison, Wisc.: Univ. of Wisconsin Studies in the Social Sciences and History, Number 20, 1934).

Perkins, Edwin J., *The Economy of Colonial America* (New York: Columbia Univ. Press, 1980).

Peterson, Harold L., *Arms and Armor in Colonial America 1526-1783* (New York: Bramfall House, 1956).

Phipps, Frances, *Colonial Kitchens, Their Furnishings, and Their Gardens* (New York: Hawthorn Books, Inc., 1972).

Pickering, Ernest, *The Homes of America* (New York: Thomas Y. Crowell Co., 1951).

Sloane, Eric, *Diary of an Early American Boy* (New York: Wilfred Funk, Inc., 1962).

_____, *Eric Sloan's America* (New York: Galahad Books, 1982). Originally published as three volumes: *American Barns and Covered Bridges, Our Vanishing Landscape*, and *America Yesterday* (New York: Wilfred Funk, Inc., 1954, 1955, and 1956 respectively.

_____, *A Museum of Early American Tools* (New York: Wilfred Funk, Inc., 1964).

_____, *The Seasons of America Past* (New York: Wilfred Funk, Inc., 1958).

Sumner, William G., *A History of American Currency* (New York: Henry Holt & Co., 1874).

Tyack, Norman C. P., "English Exports to New England, 1632-1640: Some Records in the Port Books" in *The New England Historical and Genealogical Register*, Vol. 135 (July 1981).

Vince, John, *Old Farms—an Illustrated Guide* (New York: Schocken Books, 1983).

Voss, Thomas M., *Antique American Furniture* (Philadelphia and New York: J. B. Lippincott Co., 1978).

Webster, Noah, *An American Dictionary of the English Language* (New Haven, Conn.: Author, printed by B. L. Hamlen, 1841).

_____, *Webster's New International Dictionary of the English Language*, second edition, unabridged (New York: G. & C. Merriam Co., 1958).